G000124023

ASPECTS OF
DEVON HISTORY

THE TORRINGTON CANAL, WITH BEAM AQUEDUCT, *c.* 1840

ASPECTS OF DEVON HISTORY

R. R. Sellman

DEVON BOOKS

First published 1962
This New Edition published 1985 by
Devon Books

Copyright © R. R. Sellman

ISBN 0 86114 756 1

British Library Cataloguing in Publication Data

Sellman, R. R.
    Aspects of Devon history.—2nd ed., rev. and extended.
    1. Devon—History
    I. Title   II. Sellman, R. R. Illustrations of Devon history
    942.3′5   DA670.D5

All rights reserved. No part of this publication
may be reproduced, stored in a retrieval system, or
transmitted in any form or by any means, electronic,
mechanical, photocopying, recording or otherwise,
without the prior permission of the Copyright holder.

DEVON BOOKS

Publishers to the Devon County Council

Devon Books is a division of A. Wheaton & Co. Ltd who represent a consortium of three companies:

Editorial & Design
G. A. Household, 15 Castle Street, Exeter, EX4 3PT. Tel: 0392-33186

Production & Manufacturing
A. Wheaton & Company Ltd, Hennock Road, Exeter, EX2 8RP
Tel: 0392-74121 Telex: 42749 (WHEATN G)
(A. Wheaton & Co. Ltd is a division of Pergamon Press)

Sales & Distribution
Town & Country Books, 24 Priory Avenue, Kingskerswell, Newton Abbot, TQ12 5AQ
Tel: 08047-2690

CONTENTS

FOREWORD

This is a revised and extended version of the 1962 publication then entitled *Illustrations of Devon History*, produced originally at the instance of the Devon Education Committee and mainly intended for the use of schools. As such, it is not a 'History of Devon' but aims only to deal succinctly with certain aspects of that history, using maps and diagrams to convey further information in a small compass. Maps re-used from the original edition may include in the 'modern boundary' the trans-Tamar Werrington and North Petherwin, since transferred to Cornwall; but as the originals are no longer available for correction, redrawing has been undertaken only when other corrections are required.

No attempt has been made at the entirely misleading practice of inserting decimal 'equivalents' for sums in shillings and pence, since the value of a present-day 100p bears no relation to that of the original pound weight of silver or of the gold sovereign, and is roughly that of the pre-1939 shilling. Metrication, particularly in historical contexts, also presents problems. It is hardly desirable, for example, to import metres into the laws of Alfred, or to disguise the familiar nineteenth-century railway gauges; and older readers may resent having to translate metric into imperial measurements. Native measures have therefore been retained, followed by a metric equivalent or near-approximation in brackets.

Apart from the new Sections 19 and 20, the text is based on published sources and is particularly indebted to the work of Professor W. G. Hoskins and to *The Transactions of the Devonshire Association*.

R.R.S.

A.D.	PER-IOD	EVENTS AND GENERAL	DEVELOPMENTS DEVON	
—200—	IRON AGE	Climate growing wetter.	Desertion of Dartmoor. Hill - Forts.	
—100—		New Immigration from Gaul.	Sling - warfare.	
A.D.				
—100—	ROMAN CELTIC DUMNONIA	ROMAN CONQUEST of Lowland Britain.	Exeter founded. Roman roads.	
		Partial Romanisation	slight beyond Exeter.	
—200—				
—300—		Saxon { raiding. Irish {	Decay of Roman Exeter.	
		Roman power in decline.		
—400—		Fall of Rome. SAXONS SETTLE IN S.E.	Kingdom of Dumnonia. Celtic Missionaries.	
—500—		Arthur. Saxon advance temporarily checked.	Migrations to Brittany. partial depopulation.	
—600—				
—700—	SAXON	Saxons Christianised. Growth of Wessex.	SAXON CONQUEST AND SETTLEMENT.	LAND CLEARING.
—800—			Minster churches.	
			X Galford Down.	
—900—		Danish Raids & Invasion. King Alfred.	Guthrum in Exeter. BURHS. See of Crediton.	
			Tavistock Abbey.	
—1000—		Second Danish War.	X Pinhoe. —Ravage. Exeter sacked. See moved to Exeter.	
—1100—	MIDDLE AGES	NORMAN CONQUEST. Domesday Book.	Castles.	BOROUGHS
		Monastic Revival.	Cistercian Abbeys.	Open Fields Enclosed.
—1200—		Growth of cross-Channel Trade.	Rise of Tin & Cloth Industries. Plymouth & Dartmouth.	
—1300—				
—1400—		BLACK DEATH.	Marginal land abandoned.	
		Hundred Years War.	French raid ports.	
			Church rebuilding.	
—1500—	TUD-OR	Monasteries dissolved. Reformation.	Prayer Book Rebellion.	
—1600—		Spanish Armada.	Devon Seamen.	
	STU-ART	Puritanism. CIVIL WAR.	X Torrington. Sieges. Pym. Plymouth Citadel.	
—1700—	MODERN	French Wars.	Development of Devonport	
—1800—		AGRICULTURAL & IND-USTRIAL REVOLUTIONS.	Turnpikes. Decline of local Industries. Canals. RAILWAYS. Fortification of Plymouth.	
—1900—		Farming Depression.	Rural Depopulation. Growth of Coastal Towns.	
		Second World War.	Plymouth & Exeter blitzed.	

THE STONE AGE AND BRONZE AGE IN DEVON

The first traces of man in Devon are Old Stone Age tools found in the gravels near Axminster, and others, with signs of habitation, in coastal caves at Torquay, Brixham, and Plymouth. The Old Stone Age covered an immense period – fifty times as long as anything since – but at its most flourishing there were probably under a hundred people in the county. Since they lived a nomad existence, and left behind them nothing but crude stone or bone tools, it is not surprising that their traces are rare.

With the New Stone Age, beginning in Britain (but not necessarily in Devon) about 4000 BC, fresh

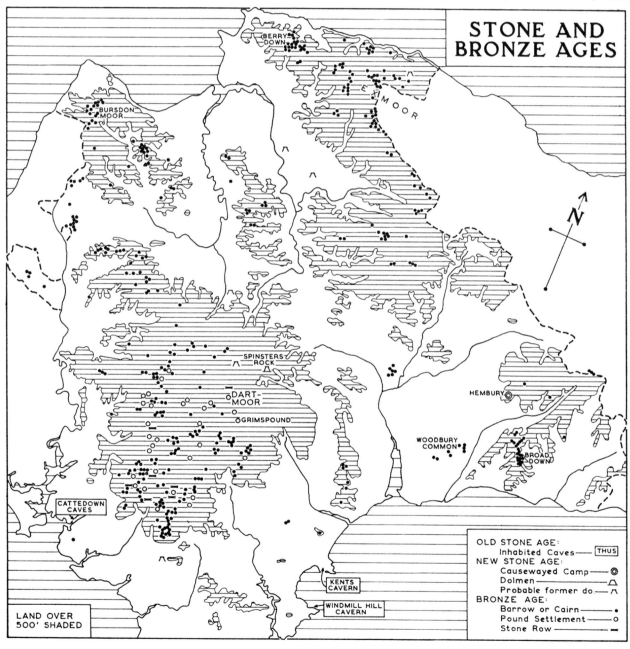

STONE AND BRONZE AGES

BERRY DOWN

EXMOOR

BURSDON MOOR

N

SPINSTERS ROCK

DART-MOOR

GRIMSPOUND

HEMBURY

WOODBURY COMMON

BROAD DOWN

CATTEDOWN CAVES

KENTS CAVERN

WINDMILL HILL CAVERN

LAND OVER 500' SHADED

OLD STONE AGE:
 Inhabited Caves —— THUS
NEW STONE AGE:
 Causewayed Camp —— ◎
 Dolmen —— △
 Probable former do. —— ∧
BRONZE AGE:
 Barrow or Cairn —— •
 Pound Settlement —— ○
 Stone Row —— ▬

arrivals from the Continent brought farming and hut-building, with a variety of new crafts, and a considerably denser population was possible. Devon, however, was much less attractive to them than the chalk lands to eastward, where they could find pasture and corn-plots clear of the forest and on well-drained soils. The climate was wet, and the valleys either swamp or forest, and Dartmoor must have been uninhabitable. New Stone Age traces are therefore much rarer than, for example, in Dorset.

To the east of the county, at Hembury, was made the most westerly of the causewayed camps which have been traced at intervals along the southern chalk hills. These peculiar earthworks, which seem to have been put up by early neolithic invaders, took the form of at least two and sometimes four concentric rings of low rampart and ditch, broken by many 'causeways'. They were not defences, since there were too many entrances, and they have perhaps been best explained as corrals for herding cattle at the autumn slaughter time, or as 'fair grounds' for periodical meetings of a scattered population. Here, and also on Haldon, have been found traces of rectangular huts which show some ability to build in timber, quite unlike the round form with conical roof which is normal throughout prehistoric times.

Long-barrows, the 'family vaults' of neolithic chieftains, are unknown in Devon; but near Drewsteignton is a dolmen or burial chamber, called Spinster's Rock, made of great stones, similar to those found in long-barrows, and the name 'Shilston' (shelf-stone) elsewhere in the county makes it probable that others once existed. All Shilston sites, as well as the Spinster's Rock, are marked on the map.

With the Bronze Age, beginning about 1900 BC, the climate seems to have been entering a long warm and dry spell, and signs of population in Devon become much more marked. Several of the 'beakers' which the first Bronze Age people buried with their dead have been found on Dartmoor. The Beaker Folk, who reached Devon from Brittany, evidently found the Moor, in drier conditions, a suitable forest-free area for their pastoral farming. They brought with them the mysterious megalithic religion, which involved setting up large stones either singly, in circles, or in rows. We shall never know just what these monuments meant, but they were probably connected with some form of seasonal nature-worship and with the service of the mighty dead. Possibly the fact that the moor was strewn

with suitable rocks made it particularly attractive for this purpose.

The stone rows, common in Brittany but rare in England outside Dartmoor, number over sixty. Many are aligned on burial sites, and may have been processional. In additional there are ninety circles, and a number of large single upright stones called menhirs. Only the more impressive of the rows can be shown on the map.

The Beaker Folk also introduced the round barrow, covering a single important (and generally cremated) burial. This remained the standard shape, with changes of detail, throughout the Bronze Age. Where these are found, we can be sure that the district carried a population at some period of its 1500 years. The map shows only the most prominent of those surviving today, but it indicates that people spread on to most of the high ground above the swamps and forests. The soils they lived on were poor, but, at least until the Late Bronze Age, cultivation mattered much less than herding. Much of Dartmoor was enclosed for cattle with 'reaves' (boundaries) made of bank and ditch or drystone walling.

Much of this pioneering dates from the Middle Bronze Age, which began about 1400 BC. People known to us as the Urn Folk, after the large pots in which they buried the ashes of their dead, built on

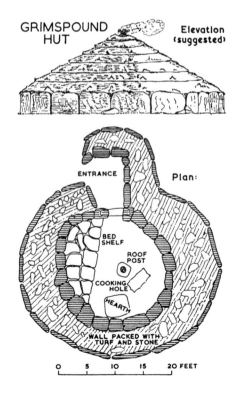

GRIMSPOUND HUT — Elevation (suggested)

Plan: ENTRANCE, BED SHELF, ROOF POST, COOKING HOLE, HEARTH, WALL PACKED WITH TURF AND STONE

0   5   10   15   20 FEET

Dartmoor over 150 pounds or enclosures, most of which contain the remains of huts. Grimspound, the most famous, had a dozen circular dwelling huts with walls of earth and rubble faced with stone, besides several others which were probably cattle byres. The pound wall seems to have been a cattle-corral rather than a defence against enemies. Many other settlements, marked by stone 'hut-circles', had no pound, but had instead an arrangement of walls between the huts to enclose corn-plots or cattle-pens. The little fields which the Urn Folk cleared of stones for their hoe-farming can still be traced by the ring of boulders, and are the earliest relics of cultivation in Britain. One expert guess is that the population of England reached some 40000 by about 1000 BC, and that might mean perhaps 2000 in Devon.

Throughout most of the Bronze Age the metal was too scarce for the everyday purposes of ordinary folk, and stone remained in use. Only in the Late Bronze Age, from about 750 BC, did bronze become more plentiful, and it was never as easy to get as iron later became, though it was easier to smelt and work. The Late Bronze Age saw the arrival in Britain of Celtic people who used a simple plough and cultivated much more efficiently, and a few of the enclosures attached to Dartmoor pounds show larger and more regular fields which may have been laid out for their cross-ploughing. This involved shallow ploughing first across the field and then up and down it, to ensure that the soil was thoroughly broken up. Mostly the newcomers preferred the chalk lands further east; and soon after their arrival the climate again began to grow wetter. By the end of the Bronze Age, about 450 BC, it is probable that the moor, and some of the other upland heaths, were again becoming uninhabitable. They were never to be cultivated again, since the iron axe allowed later pioneers in search of land to clear the forest from richer lowland soils. This fact, coupled with the plentiful supply of surface rocks on Dartmoor, explains why so much of Bronze Age date survives to the present.

Beaker and Urn

THE IRON AGE IN DEVON

The Iron Age produced most, if not all, of the earthwork forts which still crown hill-tops and cliffs in the Devon landscape. Their construction seems to have begun in the third century BC, in response to further waves of invasion, and to have continued with new building or strengthening for two hundred years. Few sites have yet been properly excavated, and the events of this period are at present less clear than, for example, in Dorset. Evidence suggests that successive invaders crossed the sea from Brittany, established themselves at first near the estuaries of the south coast, and then penetrated inland, either building forts themselves or causing the previous inhabitants to do so for protection. The earliest examples show a single line of rampart and ditch, either cutting off the neck of a headland ('promontory fort') or following the contour of a hill-top. The ramparts were often revetted with stone or turf or timber, to give a more perpendicular profile than is seen today. One such, Cranbrook above the upper Teign, was never finished, possibly because those building it were attacked and overwhelmed before they could do so.

Later forts were built or remodelled with two or more lines of rampart, following the introduction of sling-warfare from Brittany in the first century BC, and the outstanding example in Devon is Hembury near Honiton. This crowns a bold promontory with close-set double or triple lines, designed not for successive defence but to keep attackers at a distance where the defenders, shooting downhill, could reach them without being hit in return. Digging here has revealed stocks of sling-pebbles, signs of a stockade on the inner rampart, and timber platforms for slingers at the gates. This is one of a group in the south-east of the county, possibly built to resist the warlike Durotriges of Dorset, but equally possibly taken over and reconstructed by them – since Durotrigan pottery has been found in the later layers.

A peculiar type of defended settlement, found only in Devon and Cornwall, appeared in the first century BC. These were built on a slope rather than a hill-top, and had widely spaced concentric enclosures. One such, at Milber near Newton Abbot, has an almost rectangular centre, presumably for habitation. Two outer enclosures were probably for stock, while a larger but indefensible one may have been for cultivation. At Clovelly Dykes in North Devon is a similar example, probably representing a separate invasion by the same people by way of the Bristol Channel.

By no means all the Iron Age population lived in or near the forts, though their distribution on the map may be some guide to the most populated parts of the county at the time. The commonest type of settlement was probably in undefended farmsteads, and remained so throughout the Roman period; but these, unlike the forts, are difficult to trace. Most Iron Age farming in Devon was still mainly pastoral rather than arable, and many small ring-works may have served as cattle-enclosures rather than as defences.

The climate of the Iron Age was comparatively cool and wet, making the higher ground previously used by Bronze Age people no longer habitable, while the valley soils had not yet been opened up by clearance and drainage. Most of the Iron Age population seems to have lived somewhere near the 500-foot (150-metre) contour.

The Dumnonii of Devon (and Cornwall) were not as advanced as their neighbours in Dorset and Somerset, nor as most other contemporary tribes of lowland Britain. They struck no coins, and for internal exchange seem to have relied on iron currency-bars, a hoard of which has been found at Holne Chase near Ashburton. These, whose value lay in the fact that they could be converted by any smith into implements or weapons, were made in several standard sizes. Coins of Gaulish and of other British peoples however have been found at Mount Batten (Plymouth), showing that some overseas trading existed long before the coming of the Romans.

Besides the use of the rivers, inland movement was possible along the ridgeways, which followed

Types of Iron Age Fort:

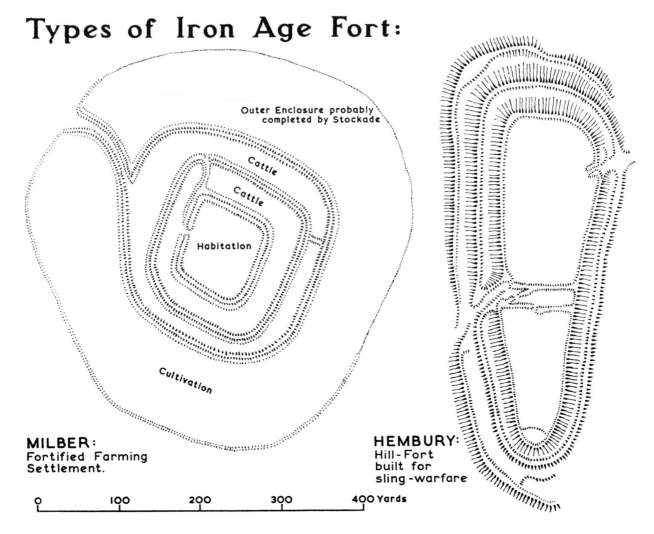

Outer Enclosure probably completed by Stockade

Cattle

Cattle

Habitation

Cultivation

MILBER:
Fortified Farming
Settlement.

HEMBURY:
Hill-Fort
built for
sling-warfare

0   100   200   300   400 Yards

watersheds, avoiding valley forests and swamps. These tracks had been in use since early Bronze Age times, and ran close to many hill-forts. Some remain in use as roads today, and one forms a long stretch of the county border on Exmoor.

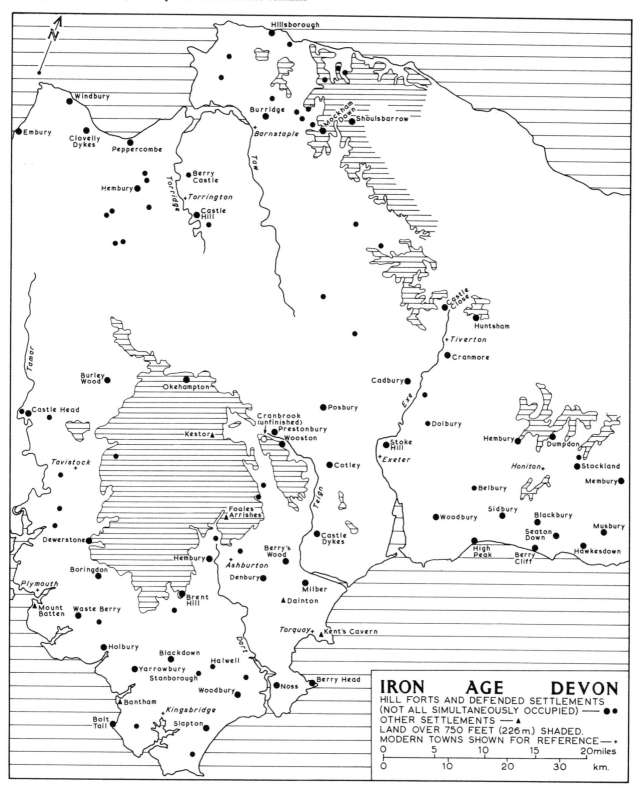

IRON AGE DEVON
HILL FORTS AND DEFENDED SETTLEMENTS
(NOT ALL SIMULTANEOUSLY OCCUPIED) —●●
OTHER SETTLEMENTS — ▲
LAND OVER 750 FEET (226 m.) SHADED.
MODERN TOWNS SHOWN FOR REFERENCE —+

3

DEVON IN THE ROMAN PERIOD

The Roman army which invaded Britain in AD 43 had first to subdue the warlike and well-organised tribes of the south-east, after which it diverged to the west, north-west, and north to complete the conquest of lowland Britain. The westward route fell to Legion II Augusta, under the later emperor Vespasian, with accompanying auxiliary troops. Sussex and much of Hampshire, under King Cogidubnus, allied with Rome and gave no trouble; but the Isle of Wight had to be conquered, and then the belligerent Durotriges of Dorset and southern Somerset who bravely but unavailingly defended their hill-forts against the long-range fire of Roman ballista artillery which swept the ramparts before a storming party went in.

Roman troops had to be left to garrison the conquered area, and it was probably only part of the legion which eventually entered Devon. About AD 47 a temporary frontier line was organised on the Fosse Way running south-westwards from Lincoln to the mouth of the Axe, its southern end marking the probable boundary between the conquered Durotriges and the Dumnonii. Penetration into Devon followed, with securing a crossing of the Exe as a first objective. The building of a legionary fort, with barracks, granary, workshops, and a massive bath-house, covering the centre of the site of the later city, followed. It was smaller than the normal size for a full legion, and possibly part of the Second remained at Dorchester to overawe the Durotriges.

No clear evidence of armed resistance by the Dumnonii has yet come to light, and they may, unlike the Durotriges, have been too thinly spread and weakly organised to resist effectively. But Roman troops spread well beyond Exeter, and eventually into Cornwall, where a fort was established at Nanstallon near Bodmin. Excavation, sometimes directed by aerial photography, is gradually revealing more of Roman military activity. Marching camps put up as temporary shelter for troops on the move have been traced at North Tawton (where a fort was shortly erected), at Alverdiscott, and north of Tiverton; and the supply-base at Topsham, serving as port for Exeter, was also probably defended, though no enclosure has yet been traced. Dorchester had a similar port at Radipole near Weymouth, which may support the suggestion that the legion was divided.

A fortlet on Stoke Hill above Exeter covered a signal-station communicating with the estuary; and a similar one was established high above the north coast at Old Burrow near the Somerset border, to watch for and report any water-borne activity by the Silures of South Wales. This was probably set up about AD 50, but the site must have been very inhospitable for its poorly-protected garrison. A few years later it was replaced by a better-built one at Martinhoe, which had timber barracks for a 'century' of eighty men. Timber barracks have lately been traced inside the ramparts of Hembury hill-fort, showing that a garrison was for a time placed there (as in Hod Hill fort in Dorset); and roads were engineered to simplify troop movements.

ISCA DUMNONIORUM

RAMPART OF LEGIONARY FORT······   LATER CITY WALL AND BANK ——
TRACED BUILDINGS, CONVENTIONALLY-■:   STREETS (PARTLY ASSUMED) ——

0   100   200   300yds   0   100   200   300m.

CEMETERIES - ©

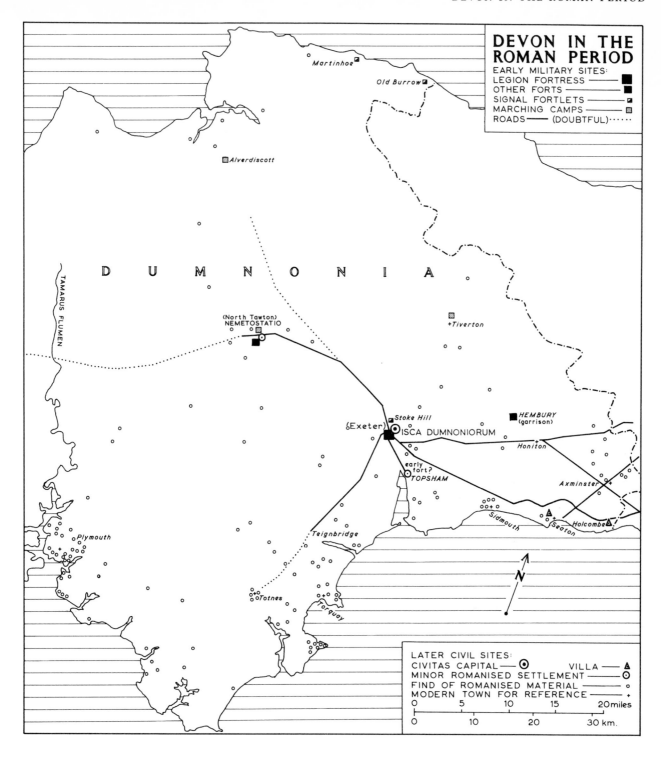

DEVON IN THE
ROMAN PERIOD
EARLY MILITARY SITES:
LEGION FORTRESS ———— ■
OTHER FORTS ———— ■
SIGNAL FORTLETS ———— ▫
MARCHING CAMPS ———— ▨
ROADS ——— (DOUBTFUL)·······

LATER CIVIL SITES:
CIVITAS CAPITAL ———— ◉   VILLA ——— ▲
MINOR ROMANISED SETTLEMENT ———— ⊙
FIND OF ROMANISED MATERIAL ———— ∘
MODERN TOWN FOR REFERENCE ———— +

In AD 60 Boudicca raised her at first triumphant revolt, and orders were sent to Legion II to march for the defence of London. The commanding legate was then absent, and the senior officer in charge refused to move. Why is not recorded, but one may guess the dispersed state of the troops and the threat of local revolt. On hearing of Boudicca's defeat, he killed himself.

The considerable garrison at Exeter, with pay to spend, must have as elsewhere attracted civilians to meet its needs, who would have settled outside the fort ramparts, and these became the nucleus of the

13

later city population. When the legion actually left on being moved to prepare for and mount the invasion of South Wales is still in some doubt, but there are traces of military occupation at Exeter to as late as about AD 75. The Legion's eventual going left a vacuum which had to be filled with some other form of authority and administration, and this was done as elsewhere by organising the Dumnonii as a *Civitas* (canton) with Exeter as their capital.

Somewhere about AD 80 most of the military timber buildings in the fort were demolished, and civilian ones substituted; but the road running around the inside of the ramparts, and the ramparts themselves, were retained, the former serving as the basis for the grid layout of streets. This was part of a general policy of 'romanising' at least the upper class of Britons, carried out with the help of money and skilled surveyors and craftsmen provided by the government. A large central block was laid out and gravelled as the *forum*, surrounded by the usual shops and offices, with the *basilica* or city hall at the northern end. The legionary bath-house (whose hypocaust pillars remain under the turf just southwest of the cathedral) was reduced in size, but retained for the use of the townsmen.

Little is yet known of private buildings in Roman Exeter, but on evidence from elsewhere we may assume the development of long and narrow houses with shop-fronts on the main streets for traders and craftsmen, and the more elaborate town houses of tribal notables occupying blocks away from the centre. The place certainly grew beyond the area of the legionary fort, and late in the second century its ramparts were levelled and new ones built to enclose well over twice the original area. There is some evidence to suggest that the gates were built in masonry at the same time, but the front of the rampart was later cut back vertically to allow the building of a battlemented stone wall.

But beyond Exeter the romanisation of the civil population was only superficial, if not entirely lacking, and Iron Age farming settlements continued almost unaffected. The North Tawton fort seems to have survived in a new form, since its name of *Nemetostatio* appears in later road-books. *Statio* meant a posting station or tax-collecting site (or both), which from its position on the route into Cornwall seems likely. The fort recently traced at Okehampton, not far away, may have been a new site for the North Tawton garrison. The only villas in Devon were at Holcombe (Uplyme) and Seaton, in the extreme south-east of the county, and they were probably Durotrigan rather than Dumnonian. There are concentrations of Roman-type material at Plymouth and (to a lesser extent) at Totnes which may suggest partly romanised settlements; but elsewhere coins, pottery, and similar objects are thinly scattered and may not mean much romanisation. Their distribution in Devon is very sparse when compared with Dorset and other lowland counties.

With increasingly oppressive taxation after the Civil Wars of the mid third century, most tribal capitals in Britain show signs of strain. As the wealthy moved out to escape the burdens of public office (including responsibility for collecting taxes), by the later fourth century Exeter shows definite signs of decay. Grass and weeds grew in the *forum*, and pits were dug in the courtyard of the baths. Coins, fairly common up to about 350, then become scarce and have not been found dated after 388. Imported *amphorae* (wine-jars) from the Mediterranean show trading contacts which may have introduced the series of plagues which hastened the fall of the Roman Empire and urban decline. Before the end of the Roman period the city was already in decay. The *chi-rho* symbol, found on a fragment of cooking-pot, shows there were some Christians by the middle of the fourth century. No temples or religious sites, apart from cemeteries have been discovered, though a number of religious objects have been found.

Isca Dumnoniorum was an outpost of romanised urban life amongst a people otherwise little affected, and geographically hardly a good centre for Dumnonia as a whole (which included Cornwall). With Exeter's decline, the centre of tribal authority of the Dumnonii moved westwards, and later rulers appear to have been based across the Tamar. Some Britons however continued to live within the city walls – if only in patched-up ruins or native huts – and continued there until expelled by Athelstan about 928; but urban life in any Roman sense had ceased by the early fifth century and long before the arrival of the Saxons.

—4—
SAXON DEVON

Some two and a half centuries elapsed between the end of Roman rule and the arrival of the Saxons in Devon. In this period the native Celtic population had been thinned by plague (a particularly bad one being reported about 540) and by a migration to Brittany sufficiently large to have given it the name it has held ever since. Those remaining had mostly

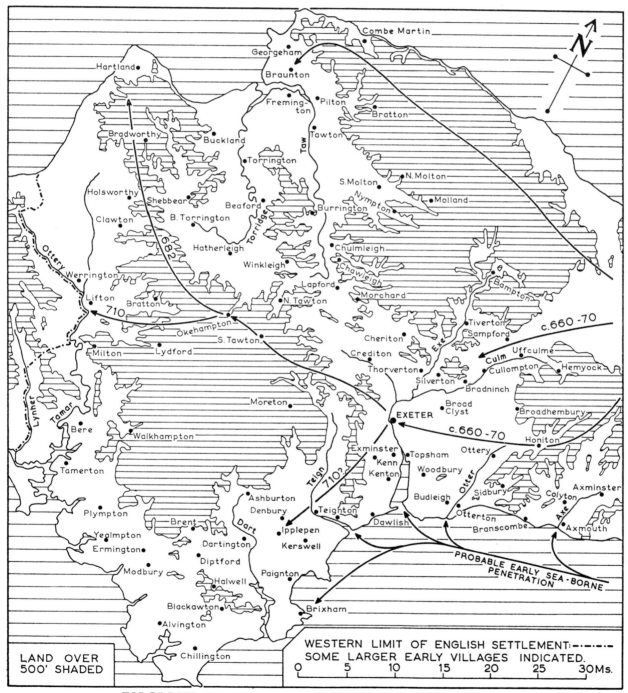

LAND OVER
500' SHADED

WESTERN LIMIT OF ENGLISH SETTLEMENT:—·—·—·—
SOME LARGER EARLY VILLAGES INDICATED.
0   5   10   15   20   25   30Ms.

ENGLISH PENETRATION AND SETTLEMENT

been christianised in the sixth century by Welsh, Irish and Breton missionaries, whose names survive in some fifty Devon parishes (and many more in Cornwall). Fragmented under a petty aristocracy, and only loosely under the control of kings based in Cornwall, they were by the seventh century ill-placed to resist the Saxon advance when it at length came; and the shortage of surviving Celtic place-names in Devon, compared with Somerset and Dorset, probably reflects depopulation.

There was plenty of land which new settlers could take without the need to fight for it. When Wessex lost its lands north of the Thames to Mercia, and looked for compensation elsewhere, the frontier barrier of Selwood Forest was at last broken by the Penselwood victory of 658 and the westward movement began in earnest. Somerset and Dorset fell rapidly into Saxon hands, and the penetration of Devon by settlers moving into the Culm Valley and along the Roman road from the eastern border soon followed. The red earth lands of the Exe valley were an obvious attraction, and Exeter seems to have been occupied without a struggle. It had an English abbot by 680.

In 682, the Anglo-Saxon Chronicle states, King Centwine 'drove the Britons as far as the sea', which implies the overrunning of the county as far as the Atlantic coast. Two ridgeway routes are possible for this campaign – either across Exmoor to Braunton or via Okehampton to Hartland, and the latter seems more probable. Early English place-names across the Tamar indicate settlement overflowing into North Cornwall. In the south, however, it is possible that the Britons for a time managed to hold the line of the Teign, and the name Denbury – 'fort of the Dumnonii' – suggests that they reoccupied this stronghold to guard the Roman road towards Totnes.

The last stage was marked by King Ine's victory in 710, probably near Lifton on the ridgeway route into Cornwall, which for a time opened up land as far as the Lynher to Saxon settlers. The coming of the English to Devon should be seen rather as a matter of pioneer settlement than a military conquest, with fighting necessary only when Celtic kings and nobles made an occasional stand. Most of the Britons no doubt stayed quiet on their farms and tried to avoid trouble.

The new settlers were great axe-men, and began in earnest clearing the valleys and gradually carving farms out of forest and waste, helped by a change to a comparatively warm and dry climate. They founded large villages, with cultivated strips in open fields such as that which, in part, still survives at Braunton (see Chapter 5). Many hamlets and isolated farms were established where land was plentiful but poor and cultivation was in separate plots from the outset.

Shortly before their arrival the Saxons had been converted to Christianity, but it took centuries for the parish system as we know it to be completed. The first step to put preaching and the Sacraments within reach of a scattered rural population was the establishment of Minsters – mother churches staffed by a body of priests and each serving a wide area. Crosses of wood or stone were set up in the localities, where a priest from the Minster officiated from time to time. Such churches have been definitely identified at Axminster, Colyton, Cullompton, Exminster, Hartland, Plympton and Yealmpton; and there were certainly more – perhaps one to each 'Hundred' (see Chapter 6). Local parishes were gradually carved out of Minster territory, as thegns built (mostly wooden) churches, but not till after the Norman Conquest did Minsters finally lose their function with the completion of the parish system. A bishop's see at Sherborne was founded in 705 for the new lands west of Selwood, and in 909 this was divided to provide a separate bishop, based on Crediton, for Devon and Cornwall. For a time later the Cornish had a bishop of their own at St Germans, but Crediton again included Cornwall before the see was transferred to Exeter in 1050.

Though Devon lay off the main lines of Viking invasion, it was repeatedly raided and sometimes invaded in force during the two long Danish Wars. The first Viking appearance was in 838, when they joined forces with the Cornish who were still smarting from their defeat at Galford Down, Lew Trenchard, thirteen years before. This odd alliance was wrecked by King Egbert at Hingston Down near Callington, across the Tamar. In 851 Danish raiders were defeated by the local fyrd (militia) at Weekaborough near Paignton, and for some time the county had peace while Viking efforts were concentrated elsewhere.

The first big invasion came in 876, when Guthrum's host, who had given their word to leave Wessex after Alfred blockaded them at Wareham, instead moved into Devon and occupied Exeter throughout the winter. Fortunately the ships supporting them had mostly been destroyed by storm near Swanage, and the next summer they were obliged to leave again for Gloucester. The final campaign which saved Wessex was fought further eastwards; but meanwhile a force in twenty-three longships attacked North Devon from across the Bristol Channel, and was completely routed at Countisbury (or possibly Kenwith).

In the breathing space which followed Alfred's great victory of 878 at Edington, burhs (permanent forts) were organised throughout Wessex as refuges and centres of resistance. Devon had four – originally Exeter, Lydford, Halwell and Pilton. The last two occupied existing Iron Age defences; and Lydford required only a rampart to protect the single approach to its promontory site. At Exeter the Roman city walls were repaired. Each perch ($5\frac{1}{2}$ yards or 5 metres) of rampart was reckoned to need four men for its defence, and areas of the county were attached to each burh to supply a man from each 'hide' of land for defence and repair. When properly maintained, the system worked well; and attacks on Exeter and Pilton in 893 were beaten off. Halwell and Pilton were not well placed to develop as centres of trade and town life, and they were soon replaced respectively by Totnes and Barnstaple as defended sites where traders could keep their goods in safety and organise their commerce. So could they in Exeter, but Lydford was too remote to become much of a trading centre and real town. In Exeter, Barnstaple and Totnes (and briefly in Lydford) there were moneyers striking the excellent silver penny coinage, under close control from London where they had to appear and collect their dies. Each coin bore the name of the maker and the town as well as, on the other side, that of the king, so any sharp practice by a moneyer could be detected and heavily punished. By the late Saxon period real town life was again emerging in three Devon centres – all accessible by water and well placed for trade.

The Second Danish War of Ethelred's reign hit Devon harder than the First. Though the thegns of the county fought off attacks in 988 with famous gallantry, the breakdown of national resistance, through lack of leadership, left the way clear for others. In 997 the Danes destroyed Tavistock Abbey

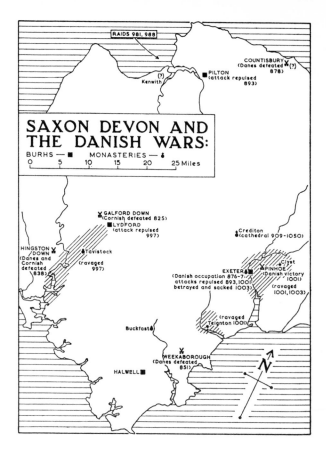

and plundered inland until checked at Lydford; and in 1001 they ravaged the lower Teign, were beaten off at Exeter, but defeated the local fyrd outside the walls at Pinhoe. Two years later Exeter was betrayed to them by Queen Emma's French steward, and sacked. Drastic as it was, the damage was local, and wooden buildings could easily be replaced, though the monastery there never fully recovered. There was no permanent check to the development of either the city or the county.

In the four centuries between the arrival of the Saxons and the Norman Conquest, nearly all the present villages and most of the hamlets had been founded. Settlement was still far from complete; but the foundations of Devon, as distinct from Celtic Dumnonia, had been solidly laid by generations of patient pioneering effort.

—5—

BRAUNTON GREAT FIELD

It was once thought that the open-field system, typical of most areas of Saxon settlement, was never introduced into Devon, despite the fact that in Braunton Great Field the county has one of the very few surviving examples. This was explained away as a piece of recent reclamation; but records show that it already existed soon after 1300, and there is no reason to doubt that it goes back to Saxon times. Further study of ancient records, and of large-scale maps, has revealed traces of open-field strip cultivation in many places, especially in the south and east of the county: but everywhere except at Braunton the system died out long before the Enclosure Acts of the eighteenth and nineteenth centuries (which in Devon applied only to uncultivated heath and woodland previously regarded as 'common'). It seems that the Saxons introduced the open-field system for their larger settlements, where the ground allowed, because it was the method they were used to, but that later generations learned by experience that small separate fields surrounded by banks and hedges were better suited to the landscape and climate and more convenient to farm.

Though open fields with strips certainly existed in many places in Devon in the early Middle Ages, there is no clear evidence that they were divided into three roughly equal blocks for crop rotation, as in the Midlands. Nor were cereals ever as important here, in comparison with stock farming, as they were over most of lowland England. There was always plenty of rough grazing without the need to leave part of the arable fallow every year, and instead parts of the common land were ploughed from time to time to give extra acreage for crops.

Braunton Great Field covers about 350 acres (140 ha.), and had originally at least 700 strips, though only about 200 remain today. It was divided firstly into blocks of about a furlong (220 yards or 200 metres) in width – the distance the heavy Saxon ox-plough could be comfortably drawn at one stretch – and then subdivided into plots one or two perches wide, making roughly a quarter or half acre (0·1 or 0·2 ha.). These were separated by a strip of unploughed turf, unlike the 'ridge and furrow' arrangement common on Midland soils and intended to help drainage. The process of buying or ex-

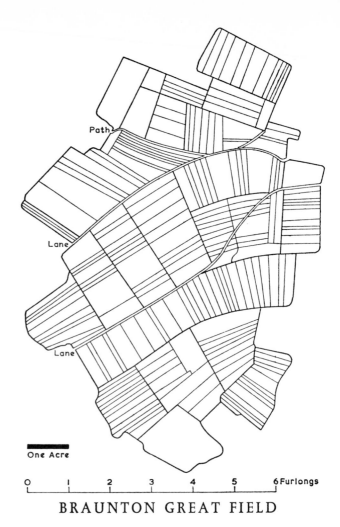

One Acre

0   1   2   3   4   5   6 Furlongs

BRAUNTON GREAT FIELD

changing strips to make a compact holding, which no doubt began early, had reduced the number of separate plots to under 500 by 1889; and since then it has gone on rapidly. As this took place, the intervening baulks or 'landshares' were ploughed out; but a fair idea of the original layout can be gained by imagining all the broader pieces redivided to match the surviving half-acre strips.

18

—6—
DOMESDAY DEVON

The Domesday record, pieced together at the Conqueror's orders from the sworn evidence of local juries, was intended to give practical information on the value and taxable capacity of estates. It was not a census, and it mentions only heads of households. Women came into it only if they held land in their own right (as three, all Saxon, did in Devon) and churchmen only if they held estates; children are never mentioned. The recorded population of about 15,500 for the county may therefore represent a total of some 80,000 – less than that of Exeter alone at the present day.

Seventy-seven tenants-in-chief (not all resident in Devon) held land direct from the King, whether as barons with many manors, or lesser men with a few or only one. In the latter group came thirteen French knights, nineteen surviving English thegns who had given no excuse for confiscation by supporting Harold or the later rebellions, and seven sergeants or King's servants who performed special duties. Three of these were crossbowmen, one an archer, and one the gatekeeper at Exeter Castle. The other two were Court officials – an usher and a hearth-keeper. 420 sub-tenants held manors, or parts of them, from a lord.

The evidence of Domesday Book is of great interest for localities, but difficult to use for firm conclusions about the county as a whole. It is sometimes incomplete, for example crediting places with ploughlands and plough-teams but no inhabitants. It shows hardly any working-class freemen outside the boroughs (such as were common in the former Danelaw), and divides the rest into approximately forty-nine per cent of villeins – holding from a manor lord a considerable area and doing service accordingly; thirty-two per cent of bordars and others of similar status – holding less land, doing less service, and probably with another occupation; and nineteen per cent of serfs – landless men who at this stage had almost slave status and were employed for their keep. The last figure is more than double the national average, and may in part represent the conquered Celtic population.

Settlement appears, as one might expect, to have been either in large compact villages, mostly then or earlier belonging to the King and going back to early Saxon times; or in hamlets – often offshoots of larger villages; or isolated farms – many of which were probably Celtic in origin or the result of later forest clearing. The highest recorded settlements, all tiny, were at about the level of the 1200-foot (360-metre) contour; but none are recorded on Dartmoor above its fringes, and there is no mention of the tin-mining which was soon to be important. Figures for live-stock, often suspiciously 'round', for what they are worth show about seventy-four per cent sheep, eleven per cent each of cattle and goats, and four per cent swine. The number of sheep implies that cloth-making was already well established. 370 swineherds are mentioned (but no shepherds – presumably that was a bordar's job), sixty-one salt-workers, and a very few iron-workers and smiths, fishermen and bee-keepers – there must have been more, simply described as bordars.

The King's own demesne lands, and those es-cheated to him as a result of misbehaviour or lack of heirs, amounted to a quarter of the whole in value, besides those of Queen Matilda who had recently died. The Church, including recent grants to a bishopric and several abbeys in France, accounted for almost another quarter; and the rest was held by tenants-in-chief or their sub-tenants.

Over ninety water-mills are mentioned (windmills not having been invented), but the great majority of these were either on the Exe or east of it. The reason for this lopsided distribution is not clear: it is not explained by relative wealth and population, since on that basis the Barnstaple area should have had more. Possibly the water-mill was a recent intro-duction here, and most of the west and north of the county was still managing with hand-querns. Some of the fisheries were evidently freshwater, and payments in salmon are recorded. Salt-pans were of great importance when meat had to be butchered in the autumn and preserved through the winter.

In population, and in productivity (except for livestock), the red earth region of the south-east led easily. Here, and in the area inland of Torbay which came second, were most of the large manors and the best soil and climate for cereals. The third area was that around Barnstaple, since the promising soils of the South Hams were not yet used to anything approaching their capacity. The poorest area, with least cereals and most cattle, was that of the Culm Measures of the north-west. As a whole, Devon was still not as developed as its eastern neighbours: there was still much room for pioneer settlement, and this was to come (see Chapter 9).

19

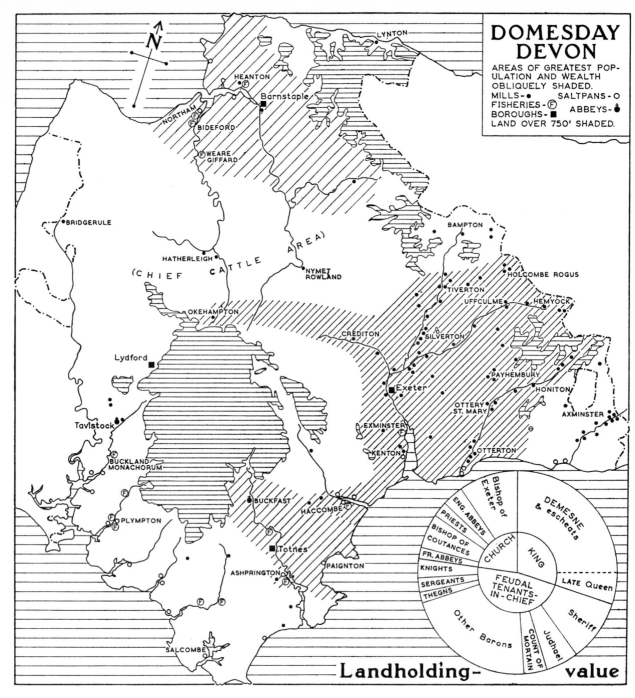

DOMESDAY DEVON

AREAS OF GREATEST POP-
ULATION AND WEALTH
OBLIQUELY SHADED.
MILLS - ●   SALTPANS - O
FISHERIES - Ⓕ   ABBEYS - ♦
BOROUGHS - ■
LAND OVER 750' SHADED.

Landholding-value

Of the four boroughs surviving from late Saxon times, three (Exeter, Barnstaple and Lydford) were in the King's hands, while the fourth (Totnes) had been granted to Baron Judhael. Exeter was much the largest, doing the same service in wartime as the other three together. 285 houses belonging to the King are recorded there, and 114 belonging to tenants-in-chief, possibly making a total of 399 (though it is not clear whether the 114 are included in the 285: some of them, at least, paid the usual burgage house-site rent of eight pence per year to the King). The number of burgesses in Exeter is not recorded; Barnstaple is credited with 40 besides 9 living outside (but whether this includes or excludes 17 belonging to other lords is not clear). Totnes had 95 plus 15 outside 'who work the land', and Lydford 28 plus 41 outside – mostly at Fernworthy. Lydford, already decaying, had lost 40 houses since 1066 which the small site of the original Norman castle there cannot account for; 48 had been lost in Exeter, mostly by the building of the extensive Rougemont Castle with its inner and outer wards, and 23 in Barnstaple which also had a castle inserted within its walls.

The distinction between burgess and villein was not as clear as it later became. In Exeter, for example, we find 11 burgesses who belong to the sheriff's manor of Kenn, and pay dues there. Several barons owned houses in Exeter: Ralf de Pomeroy

had six, and Walter of Douai ten. This gave the lord of a rural manor access to the market and to borough privileges, and somewhere to stay when attending on public business. The sheriff's manor of Okehampton also had four local burgesses, and a market and castle, and was developing into a borough.

Apart from the boroughs, and much of the royal demesne, the county had been divided since late Saxon times into 'Hundreds' for purposes of justice and administration. What they were, or once had been, 'hundreds' of is not at all clear, particularly as

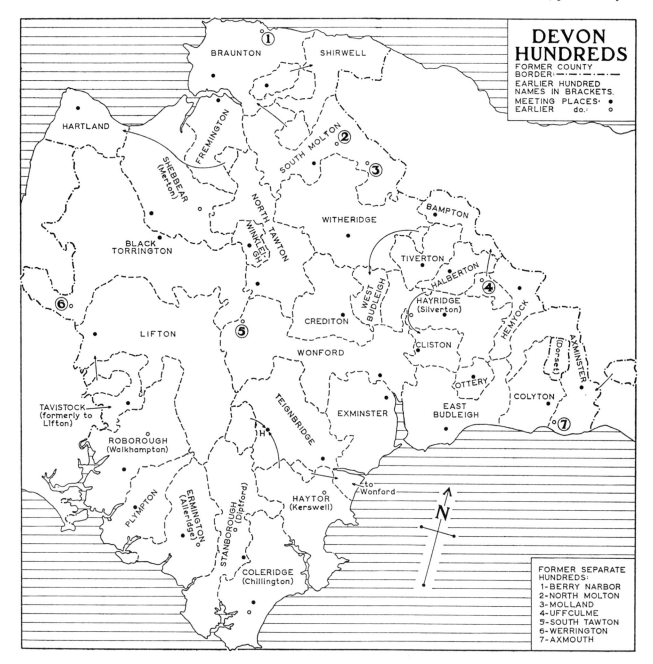

DEVON HUNDREDS
FORMER COUNTY BORDER: —·—·—·—
EARLIER HUNDRED NAMES IN BRACKETS.
MEETING PLACES: ●
EARLIER do.: ○

FORMER SEPARATE HUNDREDS:
1- BERRY NARBOR
2- NORTH MOLTON
3- MOLLAND
4- UFFCULME
5- SOUTH TAWTON
6- WERRINGTON
7- AXMOUTH

they varied greatly in size within a county and in number between counties. However, at a time when it was impossible to get people together to do all business effectively in a shire court, they served a useful purpose with their monthly meetings to hear minor cases, register land transfers, publish royal orders, and apportion taxes. In theory their moots were attended by the priest, reeve, and four respectable villagers from each place; but some Hundreds were so large, and travelling so difficult, that in practice the manor stewards often sufficed. Twice yearly, however, all adult males were supposed to turn out for the 'View of Frankpledge', when the sheriff's officer saw that they were enrolled in 'tithing' groups, responsible for each other before the law. Traditionally the meetings were in the open air, but most of the Devon Hundreds contrived to meet in places where they could adjourn to a church or hall in wet weather. The Hundred, like the shire, was a pre-Conquest survival. The shire was too useful to the king to be allowed to lapse as an effective unit; but the Hundred gradually lost its importance with the growth of feudal courts held by barons and manorial lords for their tenants, which cut right across the older system. Nevertheless it continued, if only nominally, as a division of the county well into the nineteenth century.

—7—
DEVON PLACE-NAMES

The names of places, from towns to outlying farms, throw a good deal of light on the early settlement of the county. One striking fact, in an area which the English occupied comparatively late, is that very few names of Celtic origin survive. Those which are wholly British are shown on the map, as are those containing the element 'Wal' from the Saxon 'Wealas' for Welsh or Britons. This shortage supports the probability that Devon was thinly populated when the Saxons came, though in some cases they may have renamed existing settlements. Dawlish and Whimple derive their names from local streams, and may not themselves be of British origin.

Even river names are less generally Celtic than, for example, in Dorset, though most of the large rivers and some thirty streams keep their pre-Saxon titles. Axe and Exe mean simply 'water', and Avon 'river'; and other names are mostly descriptive of the stream or its valley, such as 'swift-flowing', 'shining', 'winding', 'elm-bordered'. Walla Brook near Buckfast is the 'Welshmen's stream'.

One of the commonest ways of distinguishing a new settlement was to call it by the name of the owner of founder, with some suffix meaning 'farm' (or, less commonly, 'hill', 'valley', etc.). Nearly all such start with a Saxon personal name, and common suffixes are -*ton* (enclosure, hence farmstead), -*cot* (*t*) or *cote* (outlying farm), -*ham* (homestead), -*worthy* (farm), -*leigh* or -*ley* (wood or clearing), -*week* or -*wick* (stock farm, hamlet). -*beare* or -*bere* (wood), and -*barton* (literally corn-farm, but generally applied to the chief farm in a locality). The suffixes -*cott* and -*worthy* are distinctive of the poorer northern soils, where there were more isolated farms, but they are probably also a local fashion brought in by immigrants from Somerset. In the south-east -*hay* or -*hayne* (hedge, hence enclosure, farm) is common, and shows connections with West Dorset. Names for natural features are *combe* (valley), *berry*, *don*, and *tor* (hill), *venn* (fen, marsh), and *cleeve* (cliff or steep slope). Also frequent are *bury* (earthwork, sometimes later confused with berry), *stow* (holy place), and *buckland* (land granted by 'book' or title-deed). The spread of -*cott* and -*worthy* names into North Cornwall and the North Petherwin area, shown on

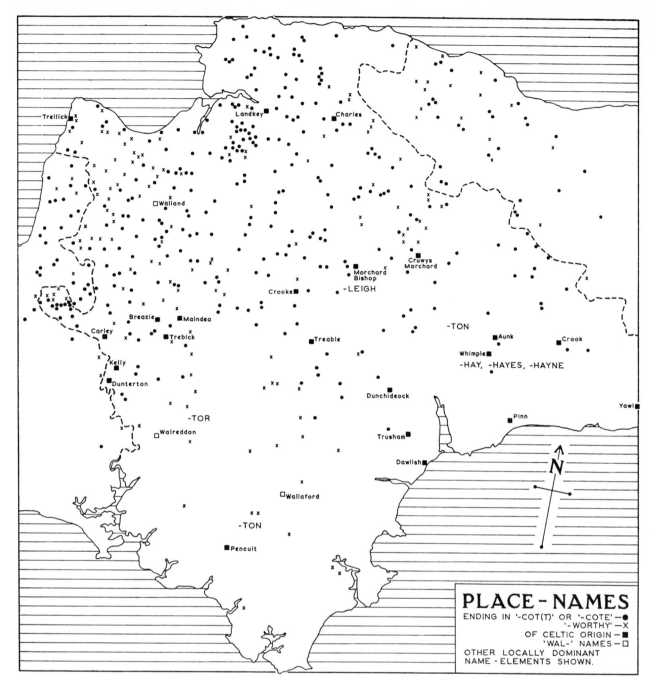

PLACE-NAMES
ENDING IN '-COT(T)' OR '-COTE' — ●
'-WORTHY' — X
OF CELTIC ORIGIN — ■
'WAL-' NAMES — □
OTHER LOCALLY DOMINANT
NAME-ELEMENTS SHOWN.

the map, is evidence for early English settlement beyond the Tamar.

The Vikings left no place-names in Devon (if we exclude Lundy – 'puffin isle'), but a few Anglo-Danish personal names appear later in Cnut's time. Norman influence is seen mainly in the addition of the names of manorial lords: Churston Ferrers, for example, is Churchtown which belongs to the Ferrers family. Other double names arose from the need to distinguish places with the same name, or to show ownership by Church or King. Examples are Mary Tavy and Peter Tavy, both named from the river on which they stand but distinguished by adding the church dedication, and Kingskerswell and Abbotskerswell.

Place-names have often changed in form over the years, and to discover the original meaning it is necessary to search early documents. In the following lists the originals are given where they noticeably differ; and names of Celtic origin are marked 'C'.

Place-names Derived from:

(a) *Personal Names*

Alfardisworthy (Alfheard)
Alston – Alfameston (Alfhelm)
Alverdiscott – Alvredescot (Alfred)
Babbacombe (Babba)
Bittadon (Bitta)
Branscombe – Brancescumbe (Brannoc – C)
Brixham (Brioc – C)
Burrington – Bernington (Beorn)
Chulmleigh – Cholmundeslegh (Ceolmund)
Croscombe – Craddokescumb (Caradoc – C)
Iddesleigh – Edwieslegh (Edwig)
Ilfracombe – Alferthingcomb (Alfred)
Kennerleigh – Kenewardlegh (Cyneward)
Knowstone – Cnutstan (Cnut)
Martinhoe – Mattingho (Matta)
Offwell (Offa)
Paignton (Paga)
Topsham (Topp)
Totnes (Totta)
Ugborough – Uggabergh (Ucga)
Werrington – Wulfredington (Wulfred)
Woolfardisworthy – Wulfrideswurthi (Wulfheard)
Worlington – Wulfrington (Wulfhere)

(b) *Natural Features or Vegetation*

Bradninch – Bradeneche (broad ash-tree)
Braunton (farm in the broom)
Brentor (steep hill)
Calverleigh – Calwoodley (clearing in the bare wood)
Challacombe – Cheldecombe (cold valley)
Chittlehampton (farm in the hollow)
Clannaborough – Clovenberge (cleft hill)
Dalwood (wood in the valley)
Farringdon – Ferndon (fern hill)
Hatherleigh (hawthorn wood)
Horwood (grey wood)
Huntshaw – Hunishawe (honey wood)
Kelly (grove, C)
Kerswell (cress stream)
Marwood – Merewode (boundary wood)
Modbury – Motberie (moot hill)
Morchard – Morchet (great wood, C)
Nympton – Nemeton (sacred grove, C, but may also derive from R. Yeo, formerly Nymet)
Pencuit – Pencoyt (wood on the hill, C)
Pilton (farm by the creek)
Prawle – Prahulle (lookout hill)
Roborough – Raweberga (rough hill)

Salcombe – Saltcumb (salt valley)
Shebbear – Sceftbeara (spear-shaft wood)
Shirwell (clear stream)
Sourton – Swurantum (farm by the pass)
Warne – Wagefenne (quaking bog)

(c) *Man-made Features or Farming*

Anstey (path up the hill)
Barnstaple – Bardanstapol (Bearda's post – marking ford?)
Charles – Charnis (chief's hall on the rock, C carn liss)
Charleton – Cherleton (ceorl's farm)
Cheriton (settlement by the church)
Cholwich – Chaldeswich (coldest farm)
Countisbury (fort on the hill, C cunet)
Denbury – Devenabury (fort of the Dumnonii, with m to f/v mutation)
Dunchideock (hill-fort in the wood, C)
Filleigh – Fillelegh (hay clearing)
Forches Cross (gallows cross-roads)
Hembury (high fort)
Huish (land of one household)
Powderham – Poldraham (farm on the polder, reclaimed land)
Salterton – Saltern (salt pans)
Shilston – Schilveston (shelf-stone, cromlech)
Slapton (slippery farm)
Sticklepath (steep path)
Teignhead – Tynhide (ten hides)
Thelbridge (plank bridge)
Twitchen (cross-roads)
Whitcombe – Wetecomb (wheat valley)

(d) *Animals or Birds*

Chawleigh – Chelvelegh (calves' clearing)
Cornwood (crane wood)
Crebor – Crewebeare (crow wood)
Rockbeare – Rokebere (rook wood)
Staddon – Stotdune (bullocks' hill)
Taddiport (toad town – nickname?)
Warkleigh – Waferkelegh (spider wood)
Witheridge (wethers' ridge)
Wolborough – Wulveberg (wolves' hill)
Yarnscombe – Ernescumbe (eagles' valley)
Yes Tor – Ernestorre (eagles' hill)

(e) *Rivers and Fords*

Bideford (Byda's ford)
Cullompton – Culumtune (settlement on the Culm)
Dawlish – Doflisc (black water, C)
Diptford – Depeford (deep ford)

Exeter – Escanceaster ('chester' on the Exe – C Isca)
Hemyock (ever-flowing stream, C)
Okehampton – Ockmundtun (settlement on the Okement)
Poppleford (pebble ford)
Shobroke – Shokebrook (elves' brook)
Stowford – Staveford (staked ford)
Tiverton – Twyfyrde (two fords)
Torrington (settlement on the Torridge)
Whimple (white pool, C)

(f) *Churches and Holy Places*

Bridestowe (shrine of St Brigid)
Halwill – Halgewille (holy well)
Instow – Jonestow (shrine of St John)
Landkey (church of St Cai, C)

—8—
RELIGIOUS HOUSES AND HOSPITALS

At the time of Domesday Book there were only two monasteries in Devon, Tavistock and Buckfast, both Benedictine houses surviving from Saxon times. Tavistock had been founded in 974, and Buckfast under Cnut in 1030. Until 1050 there had been two more, but when the cathedral was moved from Crediton to Exeter the Crediton monastery became a collegiate church; and the Exeter monks, who had never recovered from the Danish ravages of 1003, were turned out by the bishop to make way for canons.

The great continental movements of monastic reform reached England in the wake of the Normans, and houses of the Orders of Cluny and Cîteau were founded in Devon not long afterwards. The Cluniac Order was a reformed version of that of St Benedict, and laid special emphasis on elaborate worship. Its Devon houses were all dependent on outside abbeys, and apart from Kerswell and Pilton were 'alien priories' belonging to French monasteries. Barnstaple was the most important of them, and when most of the others were confiscated during the Hundred Years War, it was allowed to cut its ties with France and survive. The rest were tiny houses, often with only a prior and two monks whose business was to look after an estate and who could not carry out the full monastic life.

A much greater impact was made by the Cistercians or White Monks. Their object was to restore the manual labour which others now avoided, and to settle in remote spots where they could support themselves by their own efforts and escape the worldly complications of managing manors. They also gave the unlearned a chance of the religious life as lay brothers. Their first influence was at Buckfast, where they took over the existing monastery and began to develop sheep farming on Dartmoor. Soon afterwards, in 1136, a new house was founded at Brightley near Okehampton, with an abbot and twelve monks brought from Waverley in Surrey. This proved rather too remote, and after five years they decided to return; but on the way they were offered a much better site at Forde (then in Devon) and there they settled and built what became the most scholarly of the Devon abbeys. It was also the scene of one of the few local monastic scandals when the abbot and the bishop quarrelled and excommunicated each other in 1276. The King had to send judges to settle the fracas, and it ended with the abbot doing public penance.

In 1201 monks from Forde founded Dunkeswell, and in 1246 a fourth house was settled at Newenham near Axminster by monks and lay brothers from Beaulieu. A century later, all but three of the twenty-six inmates perished here of the Black Death; and we hear that eighty-eight abbey servants (whom the admission of lay brothers had been meant to avoid) died with them. Buckland was the last Cistercian house, being established by monks from Quarr in 1278, and also the latest monastic foundation in the county.

Difficult to distinguish from monks, except that they were free to leave the monastery on priestly duties, were the regular (as distinct from secular) canons. Except for Torre (1196) which belonged to the comparatively rare Order of Prémontré, they were all Augustinian (as were also the nunneries of Canonsleigh and Cornworthy). Canonsleigh began, as the name implies, as a house of canons, but not long afterwards the bishop expelled them by force for reasons not fully recorded, and made it over to nuns. Plympton (1121) grew into the richest of Devon monasteries, and had a 'cell' at Marsh Barton for the convenience of the brethren visiting Exeter. Like Hartland (1170) it had previously been a collegiate church or 'minster'. Frithelstock was an offshoot of Hartland which was never prosperous: it tried to mend its fortunes with a bogus pilgrim shrine, which the bishop had to suppress in 1351.

Collegiate churches, with a body of priests living in a 'college' or community, were founded in several places as enthusiasm for endowing monasteries fell off, and others, like the great foundation at Crediton, survived from earlier times. Ottery St Mary was established on a grand scale by Bishop Grandison in 1338, and included from the first a 'master of grammar'. Crediton also came to maintain a school, and both survived in the guise of Tudor refoundations. Slapton and Haccombe were both small, post-Black Death, chantry foundations, with the main duty of singing masses for the souls of founders and their kin.

In Devon as elsewhere, monastic life lost much of its earlier enthusiasm as time wore on; but only at Tavistock do we hear of really unfortunate abbots who created scandal. One was deposed by the bishop after a year's reign as a 'manifest and intolerable plunderer' of abbey property, and another was so addicted to hunting that he ran the place into heavy debt and let discipline take care of itself. An Archdeacon's Visitation of the parish church there in 1342 found that 'the vicar and clerks cannot say the Canonical Hours in the chancel, the proper place, when it rains, as the chancel has no roof. The Rectors, the Abbot and Convent of Tavistock, are responsible for these defects.' Lasting damage could be done by such, but they were mercifully rare. Before the Dissolution we find Tavistock sufficiently enterprising to set up the first Devon printing press. The tiny house of Hospitallers at Bodmiscombe, however, lived up to the warlike reputation of its Order by continual and sometimes violent quarrels over property with the Dunkeswell monks.

After the Black Death, some of the endowment which would earlier have gone to monasteries was devoted to hospitals. In the Middle Ages these were not necessarily for medical treatment: most were simply refuges for people who could no longer support themselves or were cut off from their fellows by leprosy. Leper hospitals existed outside Exeter, Tavistock, Pilton, Torrington and other places. But by the late Middle Ages leprosy was dying out, and such hospitals as survived the confiscation of chantry property became in time almshouses. Other foundations had been so from the beginning, and Clyst Gabriel near Exeter was founded for twelve aged clergy. Many hospitals had a warden who was also a priest with the duty of singing masses for the soul of the founder, and this allowed them to be suppressed as chantries.

When the Dissolution was ordered by Henry VIII, the first monasteries to go (1536) were the poorer ones with annual revenue under £200. Tavistock, Plympton, Hartland, Torre, and the five Cistercian abbeys came above this limit. Polsloe and Canonsleigh, just under it, paid to be allowed to continue. Heads of the dissolved houses were pensioned, and the rest given the option to transfer to surviving houses or (if priests) to become secular clergy. The friaries went next, in 1538, but their possessions were too small to support pensions. Friars were given small gratuities, and the option of becoming parish priests. The final closure of the remaining abbeys in 1539 passed without open opposition in Devon, and in some cases the last superiors had been deliberately appointed as likely to prove co-operative. Generous pensions were awarded to abbots and priors, and those for monks and nuns were enough to live on at a pinch. Many monks soon found employment in the secular

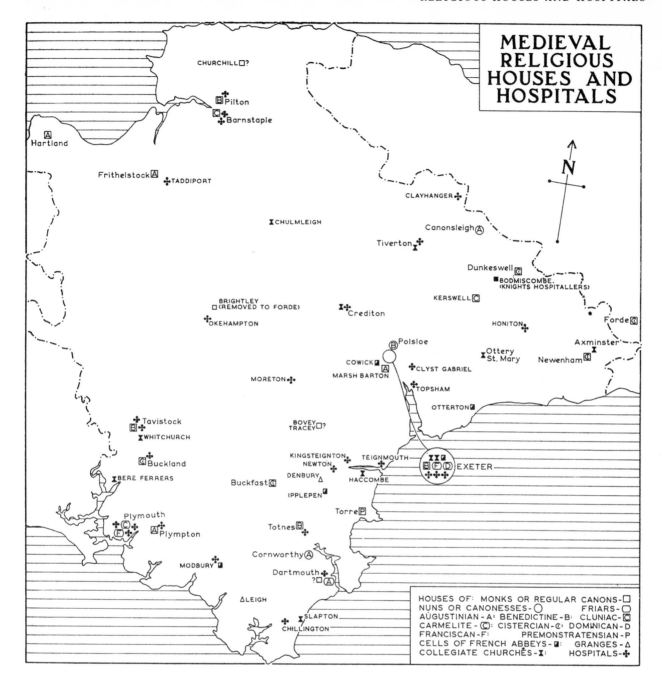

MEDIEVAL RELIGIOUS HOUSES AND HOSPITALS

CHURCHILL☐?

Ⓑ Pilton
Ⓒ ✚ Barnstaple

Ⓐ Hartland

Frithelstock Ⓐ ✚TADDIPORT

ᚷCLAYHANGER ✚

ᚷCHULMLEIGH

Canonsleigh Ⓐ

Tiverton ✚

Dunkeswell Ⓒ
■ BODMISCOMBE.
(KNIGHTS HOSPITALLERS)

KERSWELL Ⓒ

BRIGHTLEY
☐ (REMOVED TO FORDE)

ᚷ✚ Crediton

HONITON ✚

✚OKEHAMPTON

● Forde Ⓒ

Axminster Ⓘ

Ⓑ Polsloe ✚ Clyst Gabriel

COWICK Ⓐ
MARSH BARTON

Ottery St. Mary Ⓘ

Newenham Ⓒ

MORETON ✚

✚ Topsham

OTTERTON ◪

✚ Tavistock
ᚷWHITCHURCH

BOVEY
TRACEY ☐?

KINGSTEIGNTON ✚
NEWTON ✚
TEIGNMOUTH ✚

ᚷ HACCOMBE

Ⓑ Buckland

Ⓑ ✚ EXETER

ᚷ BERE FERRERS

Buckfast Ⓒ

DENBURY △
IPPLEPEN ◪

Plymouth ✚
Ⓒ
Ⓕ Ⓐ Plympton

Totnes Ⓑ ✚

Torre Ⓟ

Cornworthy Ⓐ

MODBURY ◪

Dartmouth ✚
?☐ Ⓐ

△LEIGH

✚ᚷSLAPTON
CHILLINGTON

HOUSES OF: MONKS OR REGULAR CANONS-☐
NUNS OR CANONESSES-◯   FRIARS-Ⓞ
AUGUSTINIAN-Ⓐ BENEDICTINE-Ⓑ CLUNIAC-Ⓒ
CARMELITE-Ⓒ: CISTERCIAN-Ⓒ: DOMINICAN-D
FRANCISCAN-F: PREMONSTRATENSIAN-P
CELLS OF FRENCH ABBEYS-◪:   GRANGES-△
COLLEGIATE CHURCHES-ᚷ: HOSPITALS-✚

27

Church: the last Abbot of Forde became a suffragan bishop, the last of Buckfast a Prebendary of St Paul's, and others became rectors or vicars of Devon parishes. For nuns, however, there were no such openings, and most must have returned to their families.

Much monastic property passed rapidly through the King's hands into those of reliable gentry, but estates remained burdened with pension charges as long as the former monks or nuns survived. Details of the numbers, wealth, and pensions of the larger houses were:

	annual revenue	inmates and pensions
Plympton	£912	P(£120), 17M(£10 – £$4\frac{1}{3}$)
Tavistock	£902	A(£100), P(£10), 19M(£8 – £2)
Buckfast	£466	A(£120), 9M(£$6\frac{2}{3}$ – £5)
Torre	£396	A(£$66\frac{2}{3}$), 15M(£7 – £2)
Forde	£380	A(£80), 12M(£8 – £5)
Hartland	£306	A(£$66\frac{2}{3}$), 4M(£$6\frac{2}{3}$ – £$5\frac{1}{3}$)
Dunkeswell	£294	A(£50), 6M(£6 – £$4\frac{2}{3}$)
Buckland	£241	A(£60), 12M(£$5\frac{1}{3}$ – £$3\frac{1}{3}$)
Newenham	£231	A(£44), 7M(£6 – £$4\frac{2}{3}$)
Canonsleigh	£197	A(£40), 17N(£5 – £2)

(A – Abbot or Abbess, P – Prior, M – Monks, N – Nuns)

The Dissolution had double-edged effects. It ended the local and sometimes ill-directed charity to the poor, but also put a stop to extortion from a distance. An example of the latter was the complaint of the parishioners of Wembury (in 1535) that Plympton Priory took £50 a year from the parish but provided a priest only on Sunday mornings, so that many died without the Last Sacraments, while the prior had forbidden them to hire another priest at their own expense – a problem shared with neighbouring parishes. The number of secular clergy was considerably increased, and where schools were involved they were mostly soon refounded. A major effect was a massive transfer of landed property, most of it sold or leased in comparatively small amounts, with the result of enlarging or creating many moderate estates – a factor in the 'rise of the gentry'. In Devon there was also the transfer of the property of Tavistock and Dunkeswell to the Russell family (shortly Earls and later Dukes of Bedford), in order to establish a reliable successor to the Courtenays in a sometimes troublesome county.

The wisdom of this last move was shown in 1549, when a riot at Sampford Courtenay against the introduction of the new Prayer Book in English, and other Protestant changes, developed into an armed rebellion in Devon and Cornwall. Several leading gentry, and many Catholic-minded priests, of both counties, emerged to lead it, demanding the maintenance of services in Latin, and Catholic ritual. They also, interestingly, called for the restoration of two abbeys in each county, and the return to them of half the confiscated monastic and chantry lands. Attempts by local magistrates to quiet the rebels by persuasion, and by the government by offer of pardon, failed; and the rebels laid siege to Exeter where they hoped for support from Catholic sympathisers in the city. At first Lord Russell, as Lord Lieutenant, had no troops; but he soon raised some with money provided by rich Exeter merchants and defeated a rebel force at Fenny Bridges. When the government sent him German and Italian mercenaries he was able to rout the insurgents again at Woodbury and Clyst St Mary, and raise the siege of Exeter. With further reinforcements he dispersed the remaining rebels at Sampford Courtenay and suppressed the revolt. The leaders were executed (including the vicar of St Thomas, who was hanged in full canonical dress from his own church tower). The remaining rebels eventually, after much barbarity by mercenaries, were granted a pardon.

9

TOWNS AND COUNTRYSIDE IN THE MIDDLE AGES

The four Domesday boroughs were survivals of the defensive system developed in late Saxon times, with Barnstaple and Totnes, as better trading sites, replacing the earlier Pilton and Halwell. Barnstaple later claimed a charter from Athelstan giving wide

MEDIEVAL BOROUGHS

BOROUGHS OF PRE-CONQUEST BURH ORIGIN—■
ESTABLISHED BY ACT OF PARLIAMENT————●
RECOGNISED BY ASSIZE ROLL OF 1238————●
MINOR BOROUGHS FORMED BY MANOR LORDS—•
DOUBTFUL MINOR BOROUGHS WITH MARKETS—○
STANNARY TOWNS—s   MEDIEVAL BOUNDARY

privileges and independence to its burgesses, but there is much doubt whether this ever existed. Apart from Lydford, the boroughs stood at points where rivers could be bridged and which could also be reached by sea-going vessels. Their future growth was therefore assured; but Lydford, well-sited only for defence, was bound to decay when trade became the necessary basis of a town. Okehampton and Tavistock replaced it as markets.

After the Conquest, and particularly in the twelfth and thirteenth centuries, there was a surprising growth of 'boroughs' in Devon, though many of them were never towns. The prime difference between borough and manor was the holding of land

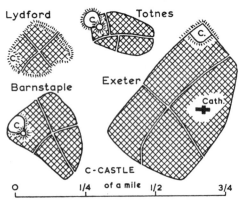

THE EARLY BOROUGHS, *comparative area and layout*

by burgage tenure, involving personal freedom, a small money rent, and liberty to sell and leave (as distinct from a villein-holding owing labour service). Many lords founded boroughs on their estates by the simple process of staking out plots and inviting settlers, in the hope that a market would grow up from which they could collect toll. Borough-founding of this kind was a 'real-estate speculation', and always included the grant of a weekly market and often also an annual fair. It did not necessarily mean that the burgage-holders achieved freedom from the lord's court, or the right to elect their own officials and act as a corporate body, which were marks of the borough in the fullest sense. When travel was difficult there was room for many market centres in an area as large as Devon, though not all places which had a market became even nominally boroughs.

In 1238 we find fourteen new places – Ashburton, Bideford, Bradninch, Colyford, Crediton, Honiton, Kenton, Modbury, Okehampton, Plympton, South Molton, Tavistock, Tiverton and Torrington – regarded as important enough to send their own representatives (distinct from those of the Hundreds) before the King's Justices of Assizes; and Kingsbridge was also by then accepted as a borough. Many other places which already claimed the title, however, were far too insignificant to be so recognised. Likewise, with regular borough representation in Parliament from 1295 onwards, only those places with considerable wealth and population for the period were summoned to send burgesses. The original list of 1295 included Exeter, Totnes and Barnstaple of the ancient boroughs, and Plympton, Tavistock and Torrington of the newer creations. Ashburton, Bideford, Honiton, Lydford, Modbury, Okehampton and South Molton were also occasionally summoned in the early days, but soon dropped out, and Torrington petitioned with success against the trouble and expense of sending members. Ashburton, Plympton and Tavistock had all grown with the development of tin-mining, and Honiton and South Molton (with Tiverton and other places) through the growing cloth industry.

So far, Plymouth and Dartmouth were conspicuous by their absence; but their rise in the thirteenth century was rapid, as their excellent harbours attracted trade from the English possessions in France. Dartmouth drew ahead first, being represented once under Edward I and regularly from Edward III's reign, and receiving its mayoral charter in 1342. But Plymouth, which had the distinction of being incorporated by Act of Parliament in 1439, later outstripped its rival. Even the larger boroughs, though of real importance, were tiny by modern standards. The population of Exeter in the Middle Ages probably never exceeded 4000, and Plymouth 2500, while the rest ranged downwards from about 1500 at Totnes and Barnstaple. Trade or industry were needed to make a town, and those 'boroughs' which failed to attract either remained, for all practical purposes, farming villages. A comparison of the map with that of the population in 1851 will show which of the medieval boroughs developed, and which remained examples of misplaced optimism. The line between a failed borough and a village which never claimed that distinction is so fine that it is not always traceable in the records.

At Exeter the Roman wall was kept in repair, and at Totnes and Barnstaple stone walls and gates replaced the earlier stockades early in the twelfth century. The only other Devon town to be walled was Plymouth, after French raids during the Hundred Years War had made defences necessary. Here the castle was built early in the fifteenth century, and a rampart, thrown up as a temporary defence, was replaced with a stone wall about 1485.

In the countryside, the period between the Norman Conquest and the Black Death of 1349 (which had later outbreaks), was one of increasing population and consequently of pressure on farmable land, resulting in much opening up of areas previously untouched. Many new farms and hamlets were established in forest clearings or on the poorer soils of moor and heath, helped by grants from manorial lords of free tenancy requiring a small money rent but not labour service. Many of the villein class could afford to buy their freedom (which was done by means of a fictitious lawsuit in which a third party claimed them and the lord gave a quit-claim), and so emerged as free tenants on previous 'waste'. But the Black Death is estimated to have cut back the population of the county to its Domesday level – perhaps from 120 000 to 80 000 – and so to have caused the abandonment of much marginal land at a time when labour shortage offered the survivors a better living on richer soils. This effect was compounded by a marked worsening of climate towards colder and wetter conditions, which set in about 1300 and lasted for some centuries. Traces of the withdrawal may still be seen in the remains of walls enclosing long-abandoned plots on the Dartmoor slopes. In the excavated stone foundations of the settlement at Houndtor near Widecombe, corn-parching ovens were found at a height and on a soil where no one would later have tried to grow cereals.

In the thirteenth century, helped by the introduction of the water-powered fulling or 'tucking' mill for processing cloth, the woollen industry spread widely into the countryside, giving rise to the common Devon surname of 'Tucker'. In the twelfth century, tinners began to work the alluvial ores of stream-beds on the Dartmoor fringes, and for a time prospered greatly. The stones and sand were smelted in 'blowing houses' with a charcoal-fired furnace and a bellows worked by the stream, and the resulting tin was cast into massive blocks in granite moulds. The Crown took its share of the profits, requiring these to be taken to the nearest 'coinage' town – Chagford, Ashburton, Plympton or Tavistock – where a corner (French *coin*) was chipped off and assayed for quality, the block weighed and stamped, and the duty paid. From the wide variations in the amount produced and the numbers working from time to time, the industry seems to have been partly if not wholly a by-employment for men who otherwise worked on the land. It required close regulation, and was overseen by a Warden of the Stannaries (Latin *stannum* – tin) who had the use of the grim prison built at Lydford in 1195 for offenders. The Stannary Parliament which met at Crockerntor is not recorded till 1494, but it, or something like it, probably met much earlier.

The Keep at Lydford

—10—

CASTLES AND FORTIFIED HOUSES

Besides the castles erected soon after the Conquest to control the four boroughs, motte-and-bailey earthworks were thrown up in several places across the open country by new Norman lords who took possession amidst a sullenly hostile English population. A motte could be raised quite quickly by the forced labour of peasants, and its steepness ruled out most forms of assault. But it took many years to settle and consolidate before its timber stockade could be safely replaced with a stone wall, and this hardly ever happened in the countryside. Most rural castles seem to have been abandoned for more comfortable manor houses as soon as it was safe to do so. Winkleigh has two, the headquarters of separate manors, and good examples remain in remote spots near Bridestowe (Burley Wood) and Wembworthy (Heywood Wood). In some places, as at Chulmleigh and near Loddiswell, Iron Age earthworks were re-used for the bailey.

Judhael's castles at Totnes and Barnstaple, and the Earl of Devon's at Plympton, are good examples of motte-and-bailey construction, with shell-keeps and walls replacing the original timber. Though the masonry at Barnstaple has long been demolished, much remains of the other two. Square tower keeps of Norman style survive at Okehampton, Lydford (the Stannary prison), and, on a small scale, at Gidleigh. Exeter still has much of its inner ward, crowning an embankment thrown up onto a natural hillock in the angle of the city wall, and surrounded by an impressive ditch. Its original but long-disused gatehouse remains intact.

Changing building-styles, with the keep replaced by massive wall-towers and gatehouses, are shown at Berry Pomeroy and Tiverton, as well as the small castle at Hemyock. The fourteenth century produced a number of fortified houses, like Compton, which could be defended against a sudden raid but were not intended to withstand a serious siege. As comfort replaced defence as the first consideration inland, some mansions were given impressive gatehouses built mainly for prestige; but on the coast the increasing threat of cross-Channel raids led to the building of artillery blockhouses covering the harbours of Plymouth and Dartmouth. Artillery castles like those at Dartmouth (adjoining an earlier castle

Exeter Castle gatehouse. The entrance (now blocked and bypassed) must have been reached by a timber bridge or ramp. The pointed openings indicate the work of Saxon masons.

built a century before) and Kingswear, were both built about 1490, and were joined by a chain across the harbour mouth which could be raised by a windlass to block the entrance.

Fort Charles in the Salcombe estuary was one of Henry VIII's line of coast defences, built in 1540, and like the others obsolete as soon as constructed. Such forts had been designed immediately before it was appreciated that concentrated long-range gunfire, as well as close-range flanking of the defences, required a fort to have straight faces and angular bastions, and not the round stone towers derived from earlier castles.

The plan of Totnes Castle shows the great motte and the heavily-ditched earthworks of the inner bailey, erected across one corner of the Saxon burh, and the stone shell-keep and walls of a later re-building which replaced the original timber. The motte dominates the town, and in Judhael's time it bore a square timber tower whose stone foundations remain visible. A small area inside the keep was roofed, but most of the living quarters, with the hall and chapel, were in the inner bailey. There are also faint traces of an outer ward, probably a cattle enclosure, but not enough to reconstruct its line. Unlike most castles of this early type, Totnes was kept in repair right up to the end of the Middle Ages: and the keep battlements, with their arrow-slits, are of late-medieval type.

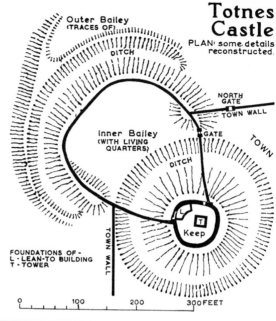

Totnes Castle

PLAN: some details reconstructed.

FOUNDATIONS OF -
L - LEAN-TO BUILDING
T - TOWER

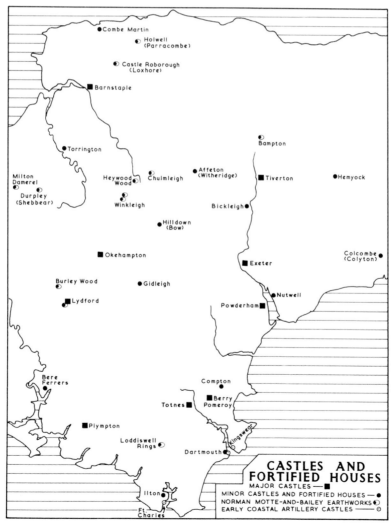

CASTLES AND FORTIFIED HOUSES

MAJOR CASTLES — ■
MINOR CASTLES AND FORTIFIED HOUSES — ●
NORMAN MOTTE-AND-BAILEY EARTHWORKS ◉
EARLY COASTAL ARTILLERY CASTLES — ⊙

ARMADA PREPARATIONS

The use of fire-signals to give warning of seaborne attack goes back at least to the final stage of the Roman period in Britain, and was part of the Saxon defensive system against the Vikings. During the Middle Ages beacons were again prepared at various times of invasion scare, as they were still against Napoleon in 1804. Before the invention of modern communications, they were much the quickest and surest method of sending an alarm over long distances.

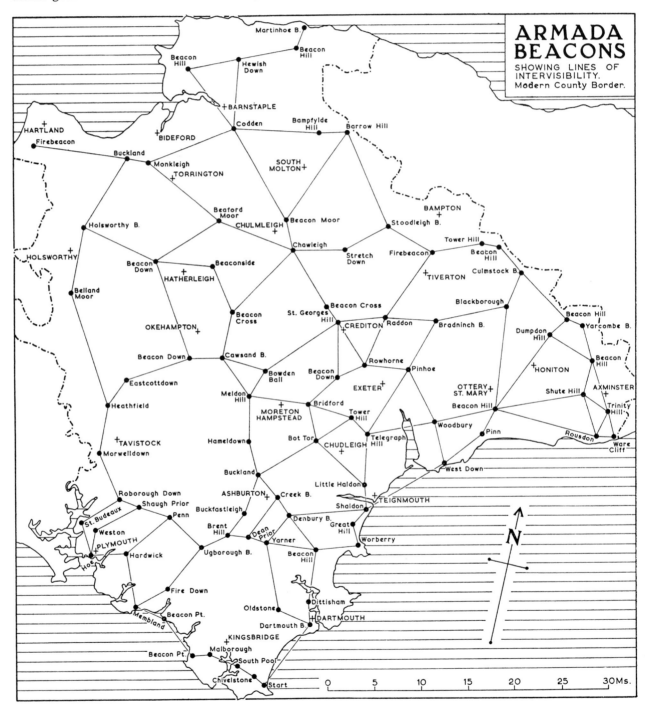

ARMADA BEACONS
SHOWING LINES OF INTERVISIBILITY.
Modern County Border.

The network prepared against the Armada in 1588 shows the system fully developed, with watching points on the coast linked by lines of sight across lower ground to the inland hills. Each spot was chosen as part of a chain, connected with those of neighbouring counties. The actual beacons were sometimes iron fire-baskets on timber supports, and sometimes low circular stone erections providing a platform with underneath draught. With prompt work, the whole county could be alerted in half an hour.

In operation, the system required every beacon to be constantly attended and watch kept on all neighbouring sites from which alarm might come. Some highly combustible material was needed to get the fire going promptly, particularly in wet weather; but heavy mists on high ground would have made things distinctly difficult. One drawback was the danger of false alarm, and the lack of means to cancel one. An over-anxious coast-watcher mistaking friendly ships for enemies, or a heath fire mistaken for a beacon, might set the whole county in an uproar which would take days to settle.

On the alarm being given, the fighting men from each parish were to assemble and take their allotted posts or be ready to march to wherever plans required. A Muster Roll survives for 1569 covering nearly all Devon, and is available in transcript. It shows that representatives of each parish were summoned and required to state on oath the names of parishioners with sufficient wealth to be separately assessed to provide arms and armour, and precisely what; and the quantity to be provided by the parish in general. Then followed the names of 'Able Men' serving as pikemen, arquebusiers (with an early form of musket), bowmen and billmen. The pike, a long and heavy spear-type weapon, was by then replacing the bill – a shorter one with a scythe-like blade; and the arquebus was replacing the longbow, since the strenuous and lengthy training needed to use the latter effectively was no longer generally undertaken.

Body armour of breastplate and thigh-pieces, with a helmet, was worn by the pikeman and billman, but the archer and arquebusier relied on heavy leather coats called 'jacks', sometimes strengthened with metal plates in vulnerable places. The bowman carried a sheaf of twenty-four arrows, and also a sword and dagger for close quarters: he could shoot five or six arrows in a minute, and if properly trained could hit his target with force at about 150 yards, while the arquebus took long to load and had a shorter range. But to fire the arquebus required no strength and very little training, while the bow needed plenty of both. The pike was some fifteen feet (4·6 m) long, and could be used with effect in defence or attack only with pikemen close-ranked and under discipline. The bill had a six-foot shaft, and was at its best in close fighting, but could be a danger to friend as well as foe if wielded in sweeping strokes.

Inland as well as seaside parishes were rated towards the cost of making and arming coast defences, the records of Morebath showing repeated payments for the 'bulwark at Seaton'; and the maintenance and manning of beacons was also a parish responsibility. Major ports were also required to provide shipping (helped by their sub-ports and immediate hinterland), though by the time of the Aramada a serious fleet action could only be fought by galleon war vessels. Levied merchantmen could only be of use as supply tenders, to carry ammunition and other supplies to the warships. The 1588 levy called for three ships of over 100 tons from Plymouth and Exeter (the latter including Topsham and Exmouth), and two each from Dartmouth and Barnstaple, besides a small swift pinnace from each of these ports to carry orders and messages.

—12—
THE CIVIL WAR IN DEVON

The origins of the Civil War lay mainly in the eleven years when Charles I ruled without calling a Parliament, and in the lack of political judgement which led him into a series of errors arousing increasing opposition. Puritanism was strong in Devon, particularly in the ports and cloth towns, and the High Church policies of Archbishop Laud were interpreted (if wrongly) as a move back towards Catholicism. Bishop Hall of Exeter was twice reprimanded for lack of zeal in harassing his more Puritan clergy. Without a Parliament to grant taxes, Charles had to resort to obnoxious means of raising money, such as granting monopolies on articles of common use like salt, starch and soap, which raised far less for him than they cost consumers and caused much irritation. More justified, if equally resented, was Ship Money, raised (at first) on ports and maritime counties such as Devon for the support of the Navy, and honestly collected and used for the purpose. The 1634 writ demanded £11 236 from the county, and most of it was, if grudgingly, paid, though Hartland produced a group of objectors. Next year, and in 1636, £9000 was demanded, and this time there was much passive resistance and goods had to be distrained and sold. The later extension of the tax to inland counties caused opposition elsewhere but lessened the demand on Devon: but by the time of the last collection in 1639, when the amounts required were much smaller, the opposition was more organised. Of the £350 demanded from Exeter, £190 from Plymouth, £150 from Barnstaple, £120 from Totnes, £80 from Dartmouth and £40 from Bideford (giving a rough idea of their relative wealth at the time), little could be raised because distrained goods were seized back or proved impossible to sell for lack of bidders.

Charles' culminating blunder, the attempt to force on the Calvinist Scots an Anglican Prayer Book and form of Church, caused a rebellion which he could not suppress, nor without calling Parliament could he raise forces even to prevent an invasion of England. Meanwhile there had been a series of bad harvests and a slump in the woollen industry – both affecting Devon – thus increasing popular resistance to taxes. The County gentry, who would normally have felt obliged to support the Crown against popular defiance of authority, instead showed sympathy with poverty and none at all with Charles' Scottish blunder which had brought on the crisis. Hence the failure of the last Ship Money demand, resulting in the neglect of the seamen impressed from the ports, which, together with Puritan sentiment, swung the Navy to the opposition.

At last, forced by the Scottish invasion, Parliament had to be called; and it at once showed more concern to attack the King's authority than to deal with the Scots whom it regarded as allies. Charles' ill-considered and abortive attempt to arrest the five outstanding leaders of the Commons (including two Devon members – Pym for Tavistock and Strode for Bere Alston) ended any hope of compromise. London was no longer safe for him and the Court, and war was inevitable. When it began in August 1642, the Devon ports were unanimous for Parliament, the cathedral city of Exeter was divided, and so was the influence of the country gentry, some leading families being split in sentiment.

Since the time of the Armada, weapons and tactics had changed; and both sides had officers with recent experience of the Thirty Years War then still raging in Europe. Bow and bill had vanished, and infantry weapons were the pike and a heavier, longer-barrelled, musket with a much greater range than the arquebus (which could also be used effectively at close quarters as a club). Cavalry now charged with the sword, reserving their pistols for pursuit, and a determined attack was usually successful – though whether they could be rallied afterwards, with horses blown and men scattered, was another matter. Fortification had evolved to make the best use of guns in flanking every face of the defences, and in the Civil War it usually took the form of earthworks laid out by engineers but quickly built by conscripted unskilled labour. Attacking it usually took the form of a sudden storm – preferably by night to achieve surprise – or of blockade in the hope of depriving the defenders of food or ammunition.

In the autumn of 1642 most of the County militia was raised for Parliament, and earthwork defences were thrown up around Plymouth, Exeter, Dartmouth and Barnstaple, with forts at Bideford and Appledore, all in Parliament's cause. But the Royalists across the Tamar, under Sir Ralph Hopton and Sir Bevill Grenville, raised the Cornishmen for the King, and began raiding into Devon. Their first attempts on Exeter in November and December were beaten off, and at the end of the year Royalist

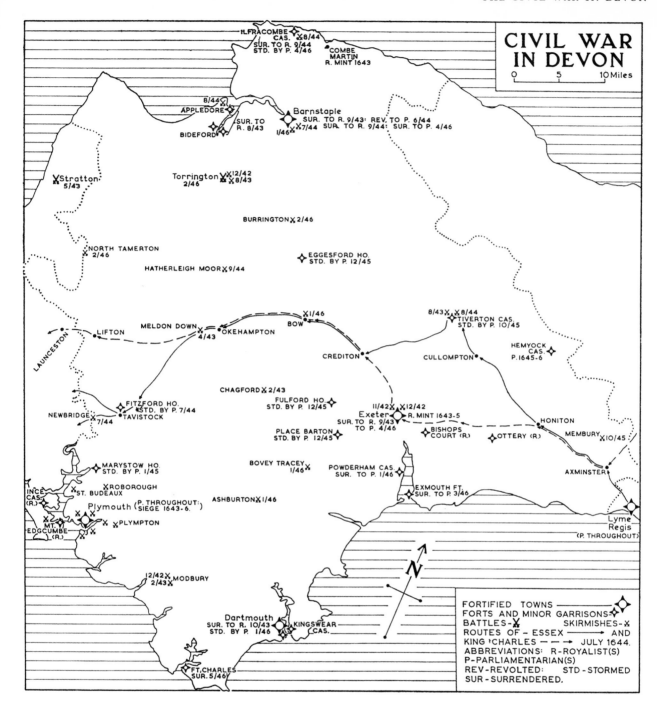

CIVIL WAR IN DEVON

0   5   10 Miles

FORTIFIED TOWNS ────────◇
FORTS AND MINOR GARRISONS-◇
BATTLES-X   SKIRMISHES-x
ROUTES OF - ESSEX ──────→ AND
KING CHARLES ── ─→ JULY 1644.
ABBREVIATIONS: R-ROYALIST(S)
P-PARLIAMENTARIAN(S)
REV-REVOLTED: STD-STORMED
SUR-SURRENDERED.

recruiting forces at Modbury and Torrington were defeated.

1643, however, saw the royal cause temporarily triumphant in the West. After a skirmish at Chagford, where a small Parliamentary force was surprised and routed, the Cornish invested Plymouth. Parliament forces mustered at Totnes, and in a hard-fought engagement at Modbury drove out the Royalists covering the siege. For two months a local truce held up operations, till in April the Parliamentarians denounced it and invaded Cornwall. Their attack on Launceston was repulsed, and the pursuit only checked near Okehampton; and a second Parliamentarian advance into Cornwall ended with the battle of Stratton which put Devon into Royalist hands for the next two years. This fierce

37

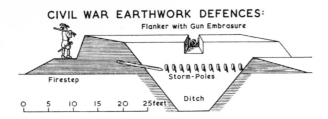

CIVIL WAR EARTHWORK DEFENCES:

fight, won by the gallantry of the Cornish pikemen against superior numbers and position, completely broke the Parliament field force in Devon and left Hopton a clear road across the county in his great campaign through southern England.

Only the fortified places remained to Parliament, and except for Plymouth they also fell in a few months. The Bideford and Appledore forts surrendered late in August, Barnstaple and Exeter in September, and Dartmouth in October. Plymouth, however, was a different matter. The Navy, which at this stage was entirely for Parliament, could supply and reinforce it at will from other south-coast bases, and the line of earthwork defences north of the town held firm against repeated assaults. While Plymouth remained in Parliament's hands the King's cause in the West could never be secure, and troops urgently needed elsewhere had to be stationed round the town to prevent the garrison breaking out. The other ports were of little use to the Royalists, since the Navy could blockade them.

1644 saw the collapse of the royal cause in the North, after Marston Moor, but a Parliamentary invasion of the South-West ended in a minor disas-

ter. The Earl of Essex, instead of aiding in a determined attack on Oxford which might have ended the war, made a separate descent on Devon and Cornwall. If his object was to capture the Queen, who had arrived in Exeter in May to bear a child, he failed when she eluded him and escaped via Falmouth to France. He pushed on, nevertheless, and crossed into Cornwall, pursued by the King, after a skirmish at Newbridge. The withdrawal of Royalist troops to escort the Queen gave the Barnstaple Parliamentarians a chance to revolt, but their attack on the Appledore fort was beaten off.

In September, Essex was cornered at Lostwithiel. He and his chief officers managed to escape by sea, but his infantry was forced to surrender, disarmed, and allowed to march off for Portsmouth. His cavalry, helped by a wet and misty night, managed to break out in small parties, one of which was routed at Hatherleigh Moor, and another was involved in a skirmish at Tiverton. In the same month Barnstaple again surrendered, and Ilfracombe Castle, which had beaten off an earlier attack, did likewise. A heavy assault on Plymouth, however, in the King's presence, completely failed; and the year ended with the situation in Devon the same as before, though elsewhere the royal cause was in rapid decline.

The defeat of the last considerable royal field army at Naseby in July 1645, by the much superior numbers of the New Model Army, left the Parliamentary generals free to mop up Royalist garrisons; but for some months they were too occupied in Somerset to deal with Devon. Not till October did

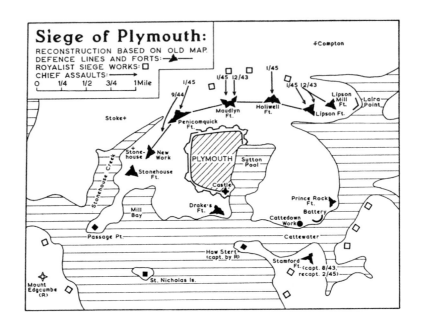

Fairfax enter the county, capture Tiverton Castle, and invest Exeter. Early in 1646 he and Cromwell began clearing operations, and rapidly fought a series of minor engagements, stormed Dartmouth, and took the smaller garrisons in the east of the county. In February came the last big fight, at Torrington, which finally cancelled the effects of Stratton. Here Hopton had only a third as many infantry, though (typically of a Royalist army) nearly as many horse, as his enemy. Fairfax arrived towards nightfall, intending to wait for daylight to view the position before attacking, but battle was unintentionally joined when his scouting force ran into opposition and was reinforced. A confused night engagement with pikes and musket-butts developed around barricades and in the streets, until after two hours of fierce struggle the outnumbered Cornish infantry broke and the royal cavalry covered the retreat. Probably by accident, the Royalist magazine of eighty barrels of powder, stored in the church with 200 prisoners, blew up and wrecked the building and much of the surrounding town. Hopton, though wounded, fought his way out with the rearguard, and those not captured fled into Cornwall and dispersed after a delaying action at North Tamerton bridge.

Next month Hopton surrendered at Truro, and all that remained was to clear up the surviving garrisons. In April, Ilfracombe Castle was stormed, Exeter and Barnstaple surrendered, and the King's Standard flew only on little Fort Charles in the Salcombe estuary, until that too gave-in a few weeks later after a four-months' blockade.

The war did much damage in Devon, though more indirectly than through actual fighting. Whichever side held power at the time demanded heavy and continual levies in cash and kind to support its troops and garrisons, and ordinary trade and manufacture inevitably suffered. The King's lack of money obliged him to leave local forces living at 'free quarter' on the country, and the less disciplined troops of both sides plundered when they had the chance.

Nor, when it was over, did things settle down. Royalist estates were confiscated, or had to be sold to meet money fines, and Anglican clergy were turned out in favour of Presbyterians or Independents. Exeter had surrendered to Fairfax on honourable terms, but after he left these were not always observed. There were soon complaints of robbery by the soldiery, and the undertaking to respect the city's churches later proved a dead letter. The cathedral was divided by a brick wall to provide separate accommodation for Independents and Presbyterians, the organ and stained glass smashed, and statuary beheaded. Its outlying buildings were all turned to secular use; and in 1657 thirteen of the city's parish churches were plundered and put up for sale on government order. Under Puritan control the city was not a happy place: the records show people fined or put in the stocks for such crimes as 'entertaining of company' or knitting on Sunday, 'for keeping company together, they being engaged to be married', 'for walking in the fields on the Lord's Day', and for allowing children and servants 'on the Lord's Day to exercise any sport, pleasure, or pastime'. A cage was erected outside the cathedral 'for the putting of such boys and others in as shall disturb the Ministers in sermon time'; and the mildest swearing brought a swingeing fine, tariffed according to social status, half of which went to the informer.

The Commonwealth was frequently at war and raised far heavier taxes than Charles had ever attempted, but still failed to pay its impressed seamen regularly. Enthusiasm for it, even in Plymouth, had waned by the time of Charles II's restoration in 1660, and Exeter celebrated with enthusiasm the end of rule by the over-godly and the military.

—13—

PLYMOUTH CITADEL

The Royal Citadel, designed by Charles II's chief military engineer Bernard de Gomme, is one of the very few surviving examples of a permanent seventeenth-century fort in England. Though its outworks were demolished late in the last century when its military value had ceased, the main building is still intact. It was built shortly before the Frenchman Vauban brought the art of geometrical fortification to perfection, and Pepys, who inspected it, expressed the opinion that 'de Gomme hath builded very silily'. Possibly one of the defects he had in mind was the carrying of stonework to the full height of the ramparts, instead of finishing them in cannonball-absorbing earth, with the guns pointing through stone-faced embrasures. Had it ever faced a siege, this would have risked the gunners being driven from their pieces by stone splinters. But it never was attacked, and the appearance today is all the more picturesque.

The main ramparts were laid out on an irregular plan designed to fit the ground on which they stood. Siege was possible only from the west and north, and here they show straight 'curtains', with projecting bastions whose flanks covered the curtain and the face of the adjoining bastion with cannon and musketry. The bastion faces could give a converging fire on any point; and two triangular ravelins, lower than the main building, covered the approaches to the bastions. A vertical-sided dry ditch protected the ramparts, and outside this was a low regular slope or 'glacis', designed to bring an assault direct into the line of fire from the parapets. On the outer side of the ditch, and sheltered by the rim of the glacis, was a covered way, which served for an outer musketry line and for assembling sorties.

On the south and east the ground falls steeply, and no assault was possible. Here outer defences were therefore not needed, and the slope was regularly scarped below the batteries covering the sea approaches. Plunging fire from the upper ramparts could be aided by the horizontal gunnery of the Lower Battery, built on the rocks at the water's edge, which also gave a protected communication with the sea in case of blockade by land.

It has often been said that the object of the Citadel, like that of a Norman town castle, was as much to overawe Plymouth as to protect it: and Charles may well have had in mind the disastrous effect of local resistance to the royal cause in the recent Civil War. Certainly it completely dominated the town, and no revolt was feasible as long as its garrison remained loyal. But in 1688 the Governor promptly declared for William of Orange, and the Stuart cause in the South-West was lost. The Citadel is still occupied by a detachment of Royal Artillery, and part of the ramparts, with guns in position, is open to the public.

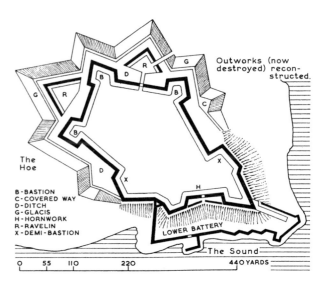

THE ROYAL CITADEL, PLYMOUTH

—14—

TURNPIKE ROADS AND COACHING

The Elizabethan Act of 1562 had made parishes responsible for the upkeep of roads inside their boundaries. It required parishioners to give six days each year of 'statute labour' on them, or to provide carts and horses, and if necessary also to pay a rate for expenses. The result was far from satisfactory, the labour being skimped and its direction more concerned with local lanes than with main roads between towns. Statute labour remained an obligation, however inadequately performed, until 1835, but when a Turnpike Road was established through a village it was normal to raise a rate and pay a 'composition' sum to the Trust to cover this requirement.

The taking over of main roads by Turnpike Trusts, empowered by Act of Parliament to erect gates and take tolls for improvement and upkeep, began in Devon soon after 1750. Up to this time (and for years afterwards) the remoter parts of the county seldom saw a wheeled vehicle, and relied on pack-horse trains for transport. The London road from Exeter was turnpiked in 1753, and soon Trusts were set up in most towns to supervise the neighbouring highways. The Barnstaple Trust came in time to control roads as far afield as Bideford, Hatherleigh, Chulmleigh, South Molton and Ilfracombe.

At first the improvement of the roads was often less obvious than the nuisance of paying toll; and not until after Waterloo did Macadam's method of surfacing, and the engineering of completely new routes, make possible the full development of coaching. Macadam gave roads a cambered surface of small chipped stones, which, when rolled, compacted into a solid and waterproof mass (but 'tar macadam' came only with the present century). New routes with easier gradients were pioneered to avoid the hills and narrow village streets of the old, and several such 'by-passes' on the roads out of Exeter remain a blessing to the motorist – though some have now themselves been by-passed. The old Exeter–Barnstaple route between Crediton and Newbridge was completely replaced by a new road along the Taw Valley, from which branches were made to Torrington and South Molton. Countess Wear bridge across the Exe below Exeter was built in 1774, and Shaldon bridge across the mouth of the Teign estuary opened a direct coast route to Torquay in 1827.

These improvements were reflected in greatly improved coach services. Properly surfaced roads allowed lighter and faster vehicles, and the new routes helped to cut travelling time. When the first mail coaches ran from London to Exeter in 1785, they took 24 hours. By 1824 this had been cut to 22, and by 1838 – with rapid changes of horses and better-designed coaches – to $16\frac{1}{2}$. This last figure meant an average speed, including stops, of ten m.p.h. (16 km.p.h.).

Two great mail routes through the county were operating by 1787, and strangely foreshadowed the later rival railway lines. One ran via Dorchester through Exeter, Okehampton and Launceston to Falmouth, and the other via Shaftesbury and Exeter through Chudleigh and Ashburton to Devonport. Cross-posts from the main towns served places off these routes; and early in the nineteenth century a third line was added through Taunton, Tiverton, Barnstaple and Bideford, to Launceston and Plymouth, giving direct connection with Bristol. Regular passenger-coach services, besides the Royal Mail, were serving all the chief towns by 1820, and in the 1830s seventy coaches left Exeter each day.

As 'Trusts', the Turnpikes were not intended to be profit-making; but few of them had a chance, in any case, of making a profit. The Parliamentary Returns of 1837 (before any railways had reached Devon), show that only five Trusts in the county, with a total mileage of 151 (240 km), were covering expenses, while 24 with a total of 777 miles (1240 km) were not. At 17 per cent and 83 per cent respectively, this was far worse than the national average of 47 per cent and 53 per cent. Funds were raised by issuing interest-bearing bonds, and all the ten Trusts in the county with over 40 miles (64 km) of road were by then in arrears with interest, the Kingsbridge–Dartmouth Trust having to pay 61 per cent, and the Plymouth–Exeter 75 per cent, of its income for this purpose. The appearance of railways, from 1844 onwards, made an already precarious situation far worse: coach services closed down at once, or after the briefest of struggles, and roads between places served by railway were suddenly deserted by all but local traffic. Inns and posting-stables, and the Trusts themselves, found it impossible to carry on; and nearly all the Trusts had been wound up before the new County Council took over the main roads in 1889. In parts which railways never reached, however, coaches survived until replaced by motor transport. One plied between Dartmouth and Kingsbridge, and a daily mailcoach ran from Bideford to Hartland, well into the present century.

But before the advent of railways, improved roads and coaches had had important effects in breaking down provincial isolation. National newspapers, as well as penny-post mail, could be rapidly carried, and the strictly timetabled mail coaches brought Greenwich time to the whole country where it had previously varied by up to twenty minutes. The upper and middle classes, at least, could travel freely without the rigours of earlier coaching. There was, however, as yet little effect on the carriage of goods, which until railways came (and in some cases afterwards), continued to rely on water transport by coastal vessels, rivers and canals.

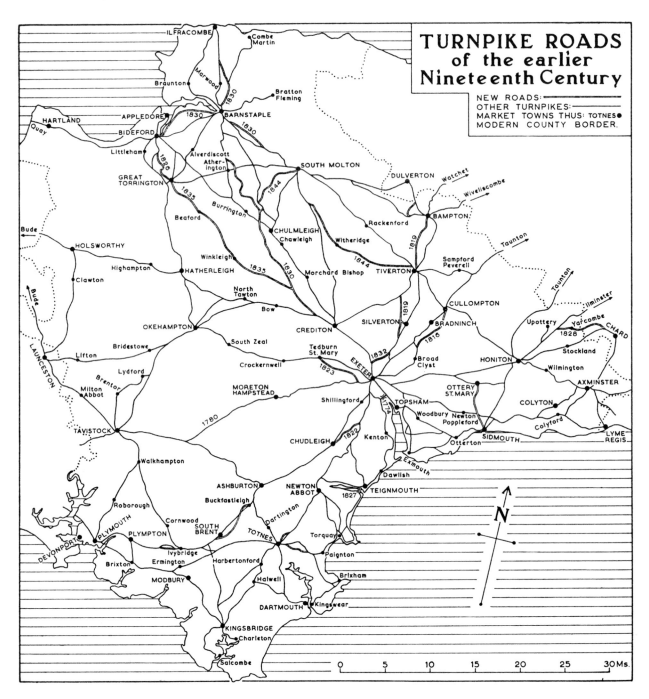

—15—
DEVON CANALS

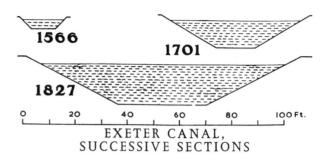

EXETER CANAL,
SUCCESSIVE SECTIONS

The history of canals in Devon is exceptional. The county produced the first in Britain to have genuine poundlocks: but most of the mileage eventually built was on the tub-boat and inclined-plane system found only in the West Country and Shropshire.

The original Exeter Canal, built 1563–6, stretched only 1¾ miles (2·8 km) from the city to just below Countess Wear. With a depth of three feet (91 cm) and a top width of sixteen (4·85 m), it could take only craft up to sixteen tons; and since very few sea-going vessels, even in Elizabeth's time, were as small as that, cargoes had to be transhipped into barges to reach Exeter by water. In 1675–7 the canal was extended a further half mile, and in 1699–1701

the whole channel was deepened and enlarged to take sea-going craft of up to 150 tons. This made Exeter again a port, and allowed West Country woollens to be shipped direct from the city and coal to be delivered to the city wharf. In 1810 work commenced on a canal which would have extended the navigation to Crediton, but after half a mile of cutting towards Exwick the work was abandoned.

The last major improvements came in 1825–7, with the extension of the channel two miles (3·2 km)

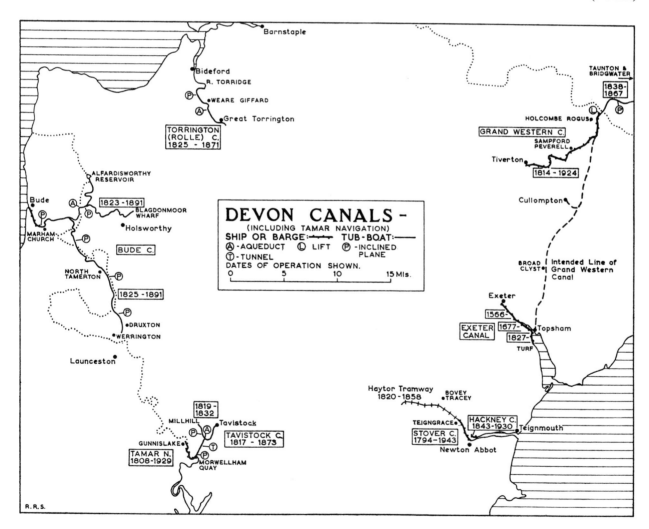

further to Turf, and the raising of the banks to give a depth of fourteen feet (4·25 m). This admitted ships of up to 400 tons, and a basin for them was opened at Exeter in 1830. For some years after this the canal saw a vigorous trade, though silting by water coming down the Exe, which fed the canal, caused problems. But the opening of the railway to Exeter in 1844 began a decline which became more marked as small sailing vessels were gradually replaced by steamers too large to use the channel. By the end of the nineteenth century the canal had ceased to pay its way, but the Exeter Corporation, as owners, kept it open as a public utility and charged the deficit to the rates. Though commercial traffic finally ceased in 1972, the canal is still maintained and used for pleasure boats, and the basin at Exeter now houses the famous Maritime Museum with craft from many different parts of the world.

The second canal to be opened in Devon, after an interval of more than two centuries, was the Stover Canal from the River Teign at Newton Abbot to Teigngrace, in 1794. This had four locks in two miles (3·2 km), and took barges of 25 tons whose main trade was carrying pottery clay for loading aboard ships at Teignmouth. In 1820 the Haytor Railway – a horse tramway using granite 'rails' with an inside flange to retain the wagon wheels – was opened as a feeder to bring granite for shipment. This fell out of use in 1858; but the canal continued to carry clay until about 1930, along with the neighbouring Hackney Canal which was opened in 1843 for the same barges.

The Canal Mania of 1793–5 produced several ambitious schemes involving Devon, but no immediate result. One such design was for making the Tamar navigable with locks for thirty-one miles (50 km) up to North Tamerton: but nothing was done until 1808, when the three miles (4·8 km) from Morwellham to Gunnislake were opened to sailing barges of 130 tons and a single lock built at Weir Head. This navigation remained in use, in a small way, till the 1920s.

Another Mania scheme, for the Grand Western Canal from Taunton to Topsham, with branches to Tiverton and Cullompton, got its Act in 1796 when the boom was already over. Not till 1810 was work started, and then not at either end, where communication was open to the English or Bristol Channels, but in the middle – on the branch between Tiverton and Holcombe Rogus where it was hoped to raise a quick trade in limestone from Holcombe quarries. This section, a barge canal of eleven miles (17·6 km) all on one level, was opened in 1814; but it cost more than the original estimate for the whole scheme, and funds ran out. For years no more was done, but it soon became clear that this isolated canal could never pay unless through communication was opened to Taunton. In 1830 the engineer James Green proposed a cut-price link by means of a small

Granite track at the Haytor tramway

canal for eight-ton tub-boats, using an inclined plane with a rise of eighty feet (24·2 m) and eight lifts with an average of twenty-four feet (7·3 m) instead of the usual locks. The company scraped together the money and, after many delays due to mechanical failure of the lifts and plane, the extension was opened in 1838. All but one of these interesting examples of canal engineering were in Somerset, but the lift at Lowdwells was just on the Devon border. It consisted of two adjoining wells of masonry, in which caissons large enough to float an eight-ton boat rose and fell alternately, connected and controlled by a chain passing over a large wheel. Motive power was the weight of an extra ton of water let into the descending caisson. Such lifts did the work of several locks, with much less loss of time and water, but they were perfected only when canal construction was already ending.

Ten years later the railway reached Tiverton, and the effect on the canal was immediate and drastic. To save something from the wreck the much-tried company leased it to the railway in 1853 (paying their only dividend out of the proceeds) and finally sold it in 1864. The tub-boat section was closed three years later, though the Holcombe-Tiverton line was still used for quarry traffic till after the First World War. After many years of neglect, in 1971 the County Council took it over, made the whole eleven miles (17·6 km) again navigable, and designated it a 'Country Park'; and since 1974 a regular pleasure-boat service has been run with a specially constructed horse-drawn boat.

The Tavistock Canal, opened in 1817, was a remarkable peice of engineering. Though its main line was only four miles (6·4 km) long, it included a tunnel of nearly 1½ miles (2·4 km) through Morwelldown, an aqueduct over the Lumburn, and an inclined plane with a fall of 237 feet (72 m) to connect with the Tamar at Morwellham. It was also built, like a mill-leat, with a slight downward gradient to provide a current for driving the mill- and mining-machinery on its course and to help the more heavily laden downward traffic. The two-mile (3·2 km) branch to Millhill quarries, opened two years later, had another inclined plane up which boats were pulled in wheeled cradles by horse-power.

This was a tub-boat canal, intended mainly for the transport of ores and quarry stone to Morwellham Quay, and the cutting of the tunnel opened up more rich lodes of copper in the heart of the Down. The great inclined plane at the lower end had two lines

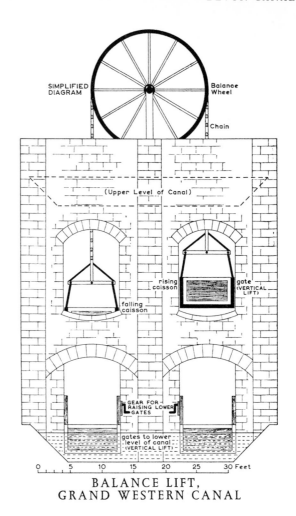

BALANCE LIFT,
GRAND WESTERN CANAL

of rails, on which ran trucks into which cargoes were transferred. These were worked up and down by a drum and chain, powered by a waterwheel. With the slump after the Napoleonic Wars, the quarry and mining business proved less profitable than had been expected. The Millhill branch went out of use soon after 1830, and the income from the main line seldom provided more than a modest two per cent on capital. After the railway reached Tavistock in 1859, trade fell off rapidly; and by 1873, when the company sold out to the Duke of Bedford for one-twentieth of what the canal had cost, it had practically ceased. Yet the canal was still to prove useful: in 1934 its channel was cleaned out and its current again employed, to drive a hydroelectric plant at Morwellham.

The most ambitious tub-boat scheme in the South-West (and in Britain) was the Bude Canal, built by James Green under an Act of 1819 and opened in 1823–5. About half of its $35\frac{1}{2}$ miles (57 km) were just across the Cornish border, but it cannot be omitted from any account of Devon canals. Its first two miles from Bude Harbour to Marhamchurch were designed for fifty-ton barges, but from that point it used four-ton tub-boats, worked in trains of half a dozen, and fitted with wheels to run on the rails of the six inclined planes. At Marhamchurch, with a rise of 120 feet (36·6 m), and at four other planes with rises of 51–60 feet (15·5–18·3 m), wheels driven by water from the upper level worked the chains: but at Hobbacott Down (225 feet or 68·6 m) Green employed the 'bucket in well' system by which a tank full of water, descending in a pit, drew up the boats with the help of bevelled gears. But the faulty iron-work of the time, and the difficulty of repairing it on the spot, led to many breakages and delays; and at Hobbacott a steam winding-engine had to be installed to take over when the water apparatus failed.

The main object of this canal was to carry shelly sand from the coast as fertiliser for the poor hill-soils, and this it did for many years. But the trade never reached anything like the expected volume; and though the company managed to stay solvent until the appearance of railway competition, it never paid a dividend. The railway reached Launceston in 1885 and Holsworthy in 1879, and by 1880 the tolls could no longer cover running costs. Finally, under an Act of 1891, the main lines to Blagdonmoor Wharf and to Druxton were closed, but the branch to Alfardisworthy reservoir survived as a water-supply for Bude.

While the Bude Canal was still under construction, the last Devon canal of any importance was engineered by James Green, on similar principles, up the Torridge to Torrington. This had a total length of about six miles (9·6 km), from its sea-lock and basin some $1\frac{3}{4}$ miles (2·8 km) above Bideford Bridge, along the west side of the river to Beam Aqueduct, and thence on the opposite bank to Torrington Town Mills. About one mile (1·6 km) from the basin was the single inclined plane, of sixty feet (18·3 m) rise, at Weare Giffard, which seems to have been identical with the smaller planes on the Bude Canal. The line was opened in 1825, and for years enjoyed a modest prosperity. A shipyard at Sea Lock built small sea-going vessels to bring in cargoes, and the chief traffic was limestone and coal from South Wales. When a railway was proposed from Bideford to Torrington, the owner of the canal, Lord Rolle, wisely decided to welcome rather than fight the new means of transport. The canal was closed in 1871, and section of its line used for the railway. The part above Torrington station became a toll-road to bypass the town (but failed as such), and Beam Aqueduct survives to carry the drive to Beam House.

No one made a fortune from canals in Devon, and most who invested in them lost heavily. Yet before the railways replaced them they were a useful means of transport for coal, lime and fertile sand, and of much more value to the districts they served than to their owners. Much of their courses can still be traced on Ordnance Survey maps, or, better still, on the ground.

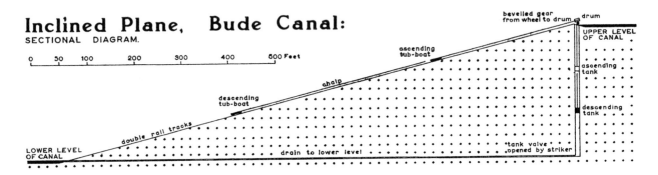

Inclined Plane, Bude Canal: SECTIONAL DIAGRAM.

—16—
RAILWAYS IN DEVON

The first railway to enter the county was the Bristol and Exeter in 1844, which continued Brunel's original line from Paddington to Bristol and was built to the same seven-foot (2·135 m) gauge. It was always closely connected with the Great Western, being leased to that company for the first five years and eventually amalgamated with it in 1876. The South Devon Railway continued the trunk route from Exeter to Plymouth, and part of its capital was found by the GWR and Bristol and Exeter Companies. Brunel was again the engineer, and the gauge seven feet: but Brunel, who made everything on the grand scale, including his mistakes, designed the line for the newly invented Atmospheric System instead of locomotive traction. This at first sight promised much to recommend it: trains would be noiseless and smokeless, running at high speeds and able to surmount steeper gradients than current locomotives, while working on a single line and in a way which made collisions impossible and derailments less likely. With single track, the lighter rails possible without the weight of engines, and less earthwork required to reduce gradients, it should be cheaper to build. If all went well it should also be cheaper to run with stationary pumping engines than with locomotives. If it succeeded on the South Devon, as Brunel confidently expected, his Cornwall

Railway would also adopt it as the only form of traction west of Exeter.

The system was ingenious, and if given time to correct its teething troubles it might well have put up a much better performance than it in fact did in Devon. The major item was a fifteen-inch (38 cm) tube laid between the rails, with the joins in the ten-foot (3 m) sections carefully caulked, and having a slot at the top closed by a continuous valve of leather stiffened and weighted by iron plates and resting on some form of grease composition to make an airtight seal. Other valves closed each end of the tube, which on the South Devon was laid in sections two to three miles (3·5 km) long between pumping stations. Steam engines worked pumps to make a partial vacuum in the tube, and the front carriage of each train had a piston which passed into the tube through the end valve and was pushed along by the pressure of air behind it, opening and closing the leather flap by means of rollers. Expresses could be run without stopping at breaks in the tube, since the train could cover the gaps under its own momentum; and with everything functioning properly the speed could be quite as great as that of any locomotive of the time.

But proper functioning depended on efficient valves and co-ordination between trains and the pumping stations ahead, so that exhaustion of the tubes began neither too late – giving insufficient vacuum – or too early so that the leather valve in the slot was over-strained. This required the electric telegraph, but Brunel provided it only between passenger stations, so that pumping had to be done

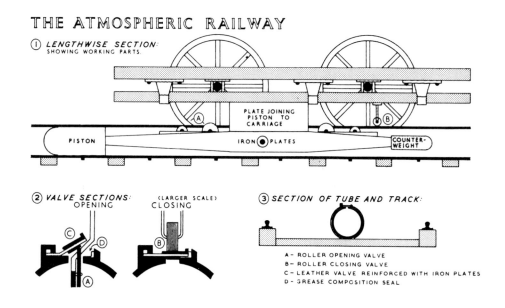

THE ATMOSPHERIC RAILWAY

① LENGTHWISE SECTION:
SHOWING WORKING PARTS.

PLATE JOINING PISTON TO CARRIAGE

PISTON

IRON PLATES

COUNTER-WEIGHT

② VALVE SECTIONS:
OPENING

(LARGER SCALE)
CLOSING

③ SECTION OF TUBE AND TRACK:

A – ROLLER OPENING VALVE
B – ROLLER CLOSING VALVE
C – LEATHER VALVE REINFORCED WITH IRON PLATES
D – GREASE COMPOSITION SEAL

by timetable and late trains meant pumps working too long and hard, waste of fuel, and valve strain.

The slot valves also gave trouble, perhaps because so much of the line ran close to the sea. This hastened the rusting of the iron plates which set up a reaction with the tannin in the leather and caused the valves to disintegrate. Given time this might have been overcome by galvanising the iron (as Brunel too late suggested) or by using rubber in place of leather, as was being tried on one section of the line just before the system was abandoned.

Further difficulties were that trains could not back (which was awkward if they overshot a station), and that shunting could be done only by manpower or locomotives; that the tube had to be broken at sidings and passing places, with danger of the piston fouling rails as it crossed them; and that level crossings were obstructed by the tube which projected above the roadway. An ingenious device for covering it with iron plates, which would automatically rise vertically when the tube was pumped, could not be used, since no one found an answer to what happened if the plates rose suddenly while a horse and cart was crossing! Underpass bridges were a possible, but expensive, alternative.

A regular atmospheric service opened between Exeter and Teignmouth in September 1847, and was extended four months later to Newton Abbot, reaching at first average speeds of sixty m.p.h. (96 km.p.h.) with light passenger trains and forty m.p.h. (64 km.p.h.) with goods. But difficulties soon accumulated: on fast trains the piston crashed violently through the end valves of the tubes, and damaged the cup-leathers which kept them air-tight; water condensed in the pipe; and the leather of the continuous valve began to decay and allow air-leaks which forced the pumps to work three times as long and hard as intended. The promised economical working therefore did not materialise – and at times the vacuum failed altogether and left a train standing, to wait ignominiously for a locomotive to get up steam and help it out. Such a breakdown blocked the whole line, as did failure of an engine or pump. Winter cold froze the leather, and without expensive treatment with seal oil it leaked or became damaged. The air-pumps proved too small for the power of the engines, which in turn had to be overworked to run the pumps fast enough to exhaust the tube; and the tube itself was too small to work heavy trains with efficient economy. Larger tubes and pumps, working at lower vacuum and so with less strain on valves, would have given better service, but would have been much more expensive to install.

By June 1848, only nine months after running commenced, the leather valve was rotting and tearing from its hinges along the whole line. This extinguished all faith in the 'Atmospheric Caper', and Brunel and the Directors decided to cut their losses and go over entirely to locomotive working. Tubes had by then been laid, and pumping stations erected, as far as Totnes and Torre; but these were dismantled without ever having been used, and all the atmospheric equipment was sold off for what it would fetch. The whole experiment cost the company not far short of £400 000, and left it with a line designed for atmospheric working with single track, gradients of 1:37 and 1:42, light viaducts, and sharp curves, such as would never have been made for locomotives. The South Devon Railway reached Plymouth in 1848 as an ordinary locomotive line: it never recovered from this bad start, and, until it was sold to the GWR in 1876, its dividend averaged only two per cent.

The North Devon line, from Exeter via Crediton to Barnstaple and Bideford, began with a 'take-over bid' from the London and South Western Railway, which hoped to use it as a link in its schemes for pushing the standard gauge into the South-West. For a brief time Waterloo got control of the Exeter to Crediton section and narrowed the gauge before completion; but the Board of Trade intervened, and the line was leased to the Bristol and Exeter and rebroadened before opening in 1851. The rest was therefore built on the broad gauge, but the LSWR (which reached Exeter in 1860) took over the lease in 1862 and laid a third rail to give through running from Waterloo. Mixed gauge continued to Bideford till 1876, and to Crediton till its final extinction in 1892. This line gave a direct rail link between Exeter and North Devon; but much of it has remained single-track, and the through service has never been good enough to break down the isolation of the north. On the contrary, with the other lines converging on Barnstaple soon afterwards, railways helped to make that town something of a separate northern capital.

The first effective intrusion of standard gauge into the county came in 1860, with the opening to Exeter of the line from Salisbury via Yeovil and Honiton. This came fifteen years after the first LSWR plans for Exeter, which produced expensive parliamentary battles with the Great Western but no positive result. In 1856 the LSWR got control of the Salisbury

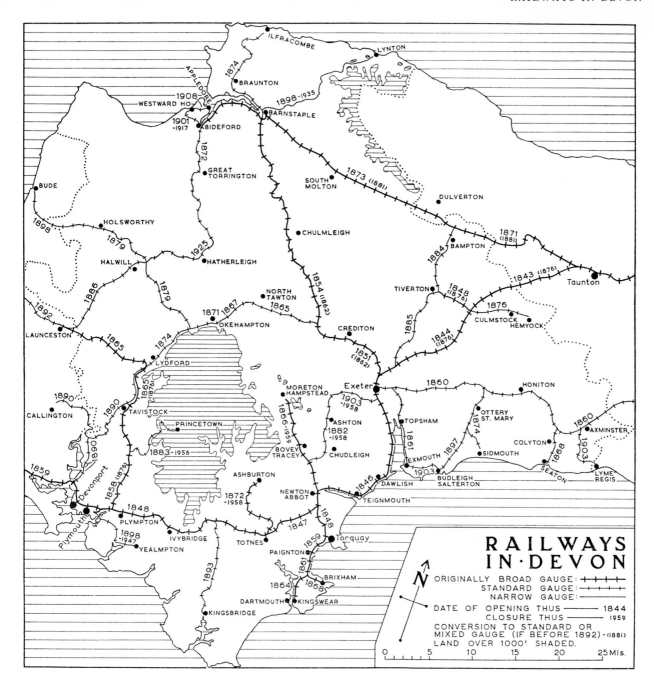

RAILWAYS IN·DEVON

ORIGINALLY BROAD GAUGE: ┼┼┼┼
STANDARD GAUGE: ┼─┼─┼
NARROW GAUGE: ──────
DATE OF OPENING THUS ─────── 1844
CLOSURE THUS ─────── 1959
CONVERSION TO STANDARD OR
MIXED GAUGE (IF BEFORE 1892) -(1881)
LAND OVER 1000' SHADED.

0   5   10   15   20   25 MIs.

and Yeovil line, and followed this with an Act for extending it to Exeter. This gave the standard gauge access to the coast resorts eastwards from Exmouth, as the broad gauge had earlier opened up the Torbay area. In both cases branches to the coast were built, often by local funds but worked and eventually absorbed by the main-line companies.

Exeter was a springboard for further LSWR advance, at first with the North Devon line in 1862 and then round the north of Dartmoor. Progress was slow, and at first held up by Great Western opposition which obliged the LSWR to undertake not to go beyond Okehampton. After it reached that place in 1871, however, this was ignored; and the line was continued to Lydford, which had already been reached from the south by the broad gauge. In 1876 the laying of a third rail on the broad tracks allowed Waterloo trains to reach Plymouth, but not till 1890 did the South Western open its independent line via Bere Alston. Requests for a third rail on the

Lydford–Launceston line were refused, to block standard gauge entry to Cornwall, and the LSWR was obliged to reach Launceston by a roundabout route through Halwill.

The spread of standard gauge lines in the South-West, with their connections to the rest of Britain, doomed the broad gauge in spite of its intrinsic merits. Many lines in the GWR system were mixed or completely converted to allow through-traffic long before the final conversion in 1892, and by that date the only unmixed broad track in Devon was the Exeter to Plymouth main line and its branches. The Paddington to Exeter line had been mixed since 1876. The nuisance of having two gauges and sets of rolling-stock on one railway system was so great that the broad gauge had to go, and the remaining track was narrowed in one hectic weekend in May 1892.

The Great Western and LSWR Companies between them came to absorb or dominate nearly all the Devon lines, but there were some interesting if financially disastrous exceptions. One was the Lynton and Barnstaple, built by a local company to the $1'11\frac{1}{2}''$ (60 cm) gauge. The cost was far greater, and the traffic far less, than had been expected, and for fifteen years after the opening in 1898 it paid no dividend at all. For another eight it managed to pay $\frac{1}{2}\%$, and then with bus competition it again ran at a loss. The company was lucky to sell out to the newly constituted Southern Railway in 1923, for a quarter of what the line had cost. The Southern in turn tried, and failed, to attract enough traffic, and the line was finally closed and dismantled in 1935. Though unpractical, it was delightful; and had it survived a little longer it would almost certainly, like similar lines, have been taken over and kept alive by volunteer enthusiasts.

The Bideford–Westward Ho!–Appledore line had a very brief existence. It was not completed to Appledore till 1908, and was a disastrous failure from the start. In 1917 the Government commandeered its track for use behind the battlefronts in France, and its rolling-stock was moved on to the main line (with which it had had no connection) by a temporary track laid across Bideford Bridge.

The effect of railways in Devon has been described by one authority as the greatest revolution since the Black Death, and for many smaller places the result was oddly similar. The county as a whole benefited by being brought into close touch with national life, and by the chance to develop holiday resorts, horticulture and dairy-farming to offset the decline in local industry and the slump in cereal production that came with trans-Atlantic imports. Big centres like Exeter and Plymouth grew rapidly, the latter especially as railways developed its harbours and suburbs. Coastal places with good beaches also throve as holiday resorts as soon as they had a railway connection. But smaller inland towns, which had previously been the only accessible market and shopping-place for their area, suffered when forced to compete with the attractions of larger centres. Crediton and North Tawton, for example, declined to little over half their pre-railway population – though the former has since recovered. Ashburton lost trade to Totnes, and South Molton to Barnstaple. Chulmleigh, by-passed by the railway, lost its market to Eggesford station. Much of the great shift of population in Devon between 1851 and 1951, with the decline of small centres and the growth of large ones, was the direct result of railways.

But the railway, which put canals and turnpikes out of business, has itself not proved impervious to the massive growth of road transport since the Second World War, and the much wider ownership of private cars. The map, drawn in 1961, shows closures to that date, but since then the 'Beeching Axe' has eliminated all remaining lines except the old GWR main route from Paddington via Exeter and Plymouth into Cornwall (with its Paignton branch), and part of the old LSWR main line from Waterloo – now single-tracked in Devon and ending in Exeter – with its branches to Barnstaple and Exmouth.

Two other ex-GWR branches, abandoned by British Rail, still however carry trains: the Dart Valley line from Totnes to Buckfastleigh and the Kingswear line from Paignton. Both have been taken over by enthusiastic volunteers, and are run with steam power, mainly as tourist attractions.

—17—

PARLIAMENTARY REPRESENTATION

In the century and a half before the Reform Act of 1832, and to some extent afterwards, the parliamentary history of Devon well illustrates the oddity and corruption of the old system. To the seven ancient boroughs represented in the later Middle Ages, another five were added in Tudor and Stuart times, making a total of twenty-four borough members, besides the two 'knights of the shire'. The latter were drawn exclusively from a small group of leading County families; but borough representation was manipulated by the Whig or Tory party machines, and no longer in any real sense represented the towns in whose names the Members sat. Many 'burgesses' were not even Devon men, let alone inhabitants of the towns in question.

The right to elect varied immensely from borough to borough. In Exeter all resident freeholders, as well as men admitted to the 'freedom' of the city, had a vote, and there were about 1200 of them. Barnstaple also had a burgess electorate of some 600, and Honiton gave the franchise to any resident who 'boiled his own pot'. Between them, these three accounted for two-thirds of the entire voting strength of the Devon boroughs: and since there were too many voters to be controlled, they had to be bribed. The inhabitants of Honiton, in particular,

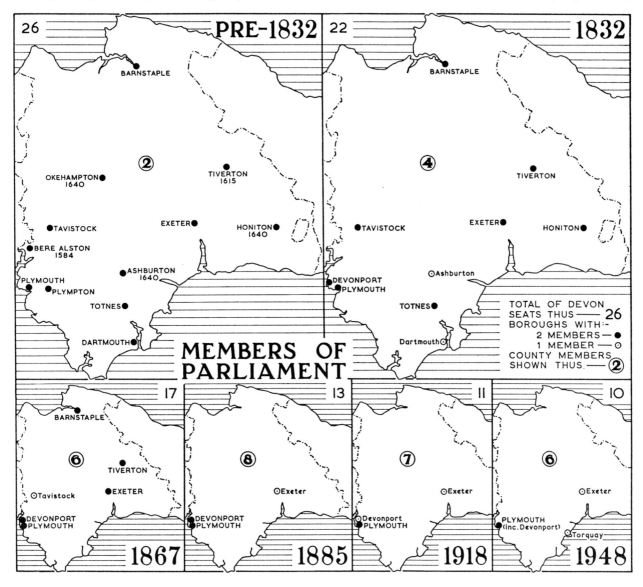

MEMBERS OF PARLIAMENT

made a comfortable income out of selling their votes, though on one occasion they were disappointed. Lord Cochrane stood for election, declaring his refusal to bribe, and so found hardly any supporters; but these he richly rewarded after the poll. Next time he stood again, with the same declaration: but the electors of Honiton, expecting the same treatment, gave him a comfortable majority – on which he thanked them and left.

Elsewhere the number of voters was much smaller, and sometimes minute. Bere Alston and Tavistock, where votes were confined respectively to holders by burgage tenure and to freeholders by inheritance, mustered about fifty electors apiece and were prime examples of 'pocket boroughs'. They provided, in Strode and Pym, two of the famous Five Members of 1642.

Dartmouth, Totnes, Plympton and Plymouth confined the vote to 'freemen', and admission to this distinction could be controlled by the Corporation or the local party manager. There were some 40 voters in Dartmouth, 60 in Totnes, 100 in Plympton, and little over 200 even in Plymouth. At Tiverton the Mayor and Corporation, who numbered 25 in all and filled vacancies in their ranks without reference to the townsmen, nominated the Members. Okehampton and Ashburton had a freeholder franchise, and mustered about 550 votes between them; but here the creation of 'faggots' – bogus freeholders, with title deeds supplied before the poll and returned after voting – could decide the result. Over the whole county, there were some 140 voters for each borough seat – and apart from the three largest electorates, only about 60.

The 1832 Reform Act was far less sweeping than is sometimes supposed, and its importance lay mainly in setting a precedent for further reform. Instead of redistributing seats according to population, it only tinkered with the old system to the extent of disfranchising the tinier boroughs and distributing the seats thus vacated to some of the larger new towns. Bere Alston, Plympton and Okehampton lost both Members, and Ashburton and Dartmouth one each, while Devonport was given two. Giving the vote to all holders of substantial borough houses swamped the most corrupt of the old electorates; but voting remained open for another forty years, and bribery and intimidation continued. At Honiton an extension of boundary gave the lord of the manor control of one seat, and Totnes kept up its tradition of bought elections, till both places were disfranchised in 1867.

The Act of 1832 left Devon with twenty-two members, including four from County divisions, but that of 1867 cut the total to seventeen. The old over-representation of boroughs, as against the countryside, was further reduced as the town seats fell to eleven and the County divisions rose to six; but not till 1885 was a clean sweep made and constituencies rearranged according to population. Of the then thirteen Devon Members, eight represented the divisions, and five the boroughs. At the same time, giving the vote to all male heads of household enfranchised farm labourers, and at last established the principle that Parliament should represent people as distinct from property. Later years saw the extension of the vote to all men over twenty-one and women over thirty in 1918, to women over twenty-one in 1928, and to all over eighteen 40 years later. The post-war growth of Plymouth has resulted in its having three seats, while Exeter and Torquay (now Torbay) have one each and there are five County divisions.

—18—
PLYMOUTH NAVAL BASE AND FORTRESS

Though Plymouth had been of naval importance since the later Middle Ages, the development of a regular naval base began only at the end of the seventeenth century. Charles II's Citadel, started in 1667, replaced Drake's fort with a much larger and better designed defence covering thirty-three acres and mounting some 160 guns to sweep the land and sea approaches; but while the Dutch remained the chief enemy, and the North Sea the main area of naval operations, there was no immediate need for a dockyard. Private shipyards in the Cattewater coped with repairs to naval vessels.

Years War, a line of fortifications was begun round the then limits of the dockyard and town; but though further work was done during the Napoleonic Wars, they were not fully completed till the mid nineteenth century. New batteries were built covering the sea approaches during the American war, when command of the sea was temporarily lost in 1781, and several more during the Napoleonic invasion scare of 1804. Not till the 1860s, however, was Plymouth (together with Portsmouth, Chatham and Dover) given serious defences capable of withstanding a siege. The appearance of the ironclad warship at this time, and of new and much more powerful types of naval gun, temporarily wiped out much of Britain's naval superiority and made Napoleon III's growing fleet appear more of a threat than it actually was.

Palmerston's defences were designed to prevent the French seizing the Channel Fleet's bases by a

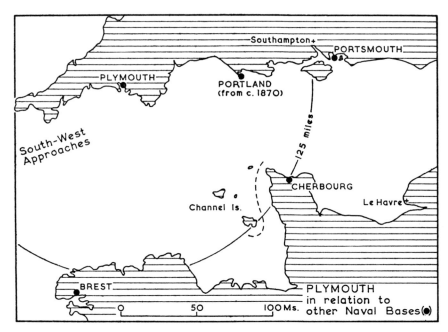

PLYMOUTH in relation to other Naval Bases (●)

But after the Revolution of 1688, France became the chief threat and remained so for two centuries. In 1686 the aggressively minded Louis XIV began to develop a naval port at Cherbourg, in addition to that already in use at Brest, and an English base further west than Portsmouth was essential. At first there was some idea of choosing Dartmouth, or a Plymouth site at Turnchapel, but in 1691 began the construction of the first dock on the Hamoaze. Extensions throughout the eighteenth century, and the growth of a new naval town, made 'Plymouth Dock' larger than Plymouth itself by the time of Napoleon. In 1756, with the outbreak of the Seven

sudden landing circumventing the harbour batteries. The original plan, made in 1859, envisaged more works than were ever built, including six forts and a rampart to cover the approach to Saltash. After Palmerston's death in 1865 the very different Gladstone, with his dislike of military expenditure, took over, and the Saltash side was left undefended – leaving a dangerous gap from which the dockyard might have been bombarded. An intended rampart and fort between Scraesdon and Tregantle was also dropped. Most of the major works actually built were ready by 1870, and construction of seaward batteries continued into the 1890s; but the landward

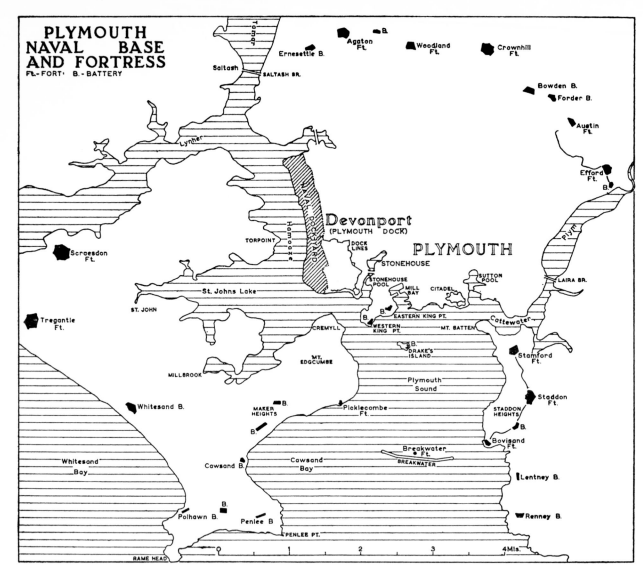

defences were never armed with the guns they were intended to mount. Palmerston's commission had estimated for 742 heavy guns and a standing garrison of 15,000, but this was far too much for Gladstone. The sea approaches were, however, effectively covered without delay by massive casemated forts at Picklecombe and Bovisand, and by the Breakwater Fort – armoured, like those in the Solent, with four layers of thick iron plate with iron concrete between them. The landward forts took the typical form of the time, with vertical ditches covered against assault by fire from caponiers projecting below rampart level at the corners, and counterscarp galleries, with mountings for the main armament emplaced in massive ramparts of tipped earth, and magazines and living quarters similarly bomb-proofed. In fact, the decline of French naval power and the effective re-establishment of British naval supremacy after 1870 removed any threat of a major French landing, and justified the refusal to arm the landward forts.

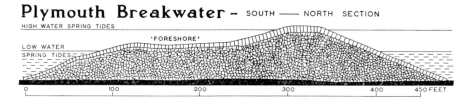

Plymouth Breakwater – SOUTH —— NORTH SECTION

During the eighteenth-century wars, and particularly during those of the French Revolution and Napoleon, Plymouth was a vital base for blockading the opposing French coast and ports: but it was never a safe refuge in a southerly gale. Fleets by this time were too large to lie up in the Hamoaze, and would in any case have taken too long to get to sea through the narrow entrance on a sudden alarm. Admirals often preferred Torbay to Plymouth Sound, but there they were equally exposed to a storm from the east. The only effective answer was to construct an artificial harbour; but the size and difficulty of the project were daunting, and there were conflicting opinions on where it could best be built. In 1806 the elder Rennie recommended a breakwater right in the middle of the Sound, leaving channels at either side which the increased tidal scour would keep clear, but the work was not started till 1812, when the war was nearly over. Three and a half million tons of limestone blocks from the Oreston quarries were ferried out in barges, dumped between buoys marking the line, and left to be compounded into a solid mass by the force of the waves. The work was not finished till 1848, but it was already far enough advanced to be admired by Napoleon when he reached Plymouth as a captive in the *Bellerophon* after Waterloo. Experience of heavy storms during construction made a more gentle shelving seaward slope on the breakwater necessary, and a 'foreshore' was added in front of the crest to break the force of the waves. Finally completed, and cased with squared dovetailed blocks, it proved able to resist all weathers. At last, the Sound was safe with the wind in any quarter.

The awkward period when ships carried steam-engines as well as sail made further dockyard extensions necessary, as did later the increasing size of vessels and specialisation into different types. The end of the old rivalry with France, and the outbreak of war with Germany in 1914, transferred the main area of heavy-ship operations back to the North Sea, and robbed Plymouth of much of its value as a battleship and cruiser base. Instead, the development of submarine warfare against the vital supply lines in the South-Western Approaches gave it a new role in escort and anti-submarine work, which it kept in the war of 1939–45.

PLYMOUTH – SUTTON POOL AND PART OF THE CITADEL, *c.* 1840

—19—
THE POOR LAW

The Poor Law Act of 1601 made each parish responsible for setting the able-bodied unemployed to work, and for relieving those unable to support themselves, and required that Overseers be appointed to see this done and to raise for the purpose a rate on the occupiers of property. But people did not always, by any means, stay in the place where they were born, and the question inevitably arose of which parish was responsible for incomers. Hence the 'Law of Settlement', and the mass of information in Devon parish records on the examination of such people to find where they belonged, and on their removal if necessary to the place where they were 'settled'. The examination records show great numbers of brief working-class 'biographies', with movements, wages, and many other details of people otherwise unknown to history.

Successive Acts, from 1662 onwards, attempted to deal with this problem, and from them, and from the cases locally recorded, it emerges that a legitimate child got the Settlement of its father, an illegitimate one (until 1834) in its parish of birth, and a wife that of her husband. Settlement in another parish could be gained by serving an apprenticeship (the last

complete forty days of it deciding where), by completing a year's contract of living-in service, or by occupying and paying rates on a property worth £10 a year. Lawyers did very well out of arguing hard cases, and sometimes odd decisions followed. In 1833, for example, an East Budleigh boy apprenticed to a Topsham shipmaster was held to have acquired a Settlement in Kenton (with which place he had no connection whatever), because the vessel had lain for forty days in 'the Bight of Exmouth Harbour' – notionally in Kenton parish.

Parish Overseers, appointed in rotation for a year at a time from among the major property occupiers, had varied and arduous responsibilities. They provided out-relief in cash and clothing to the poor, and buried pauper dead (but had the right to claim their goods, if any, as parish property). They saw that the children of the poor were 'apprenticed' at an early age (often eight or nine) to local occupiers in rotation, nearly all boys to 'husbandry' – farm work – and girls to 'housewifery' – domestic service, in both cases for maintenance only. Boys were bound till twenty-four until 1778, and then till twenty-one; and girls till twenty-one (or, after 1734, till marriage if earlier). This relieved the Poor Rate, as well as poor parents, from the cost of maintaining children.

In the mid eighteenth century there was a widespread movement to establish parish workhouses, in the hope of reducing costs by making entry a condi-

CHERITON FITZPAINE PARISH WORKHOUSE: 1754 DIET SHEET

	BREAKFAST	DINNER	SUPPER
SUN.	4 oz. bread, 2 oz. cheese, 1 pint beer.	8 oz. beef or mutton, 4 oz. bread, 1 pint beer, vegetables.	broth, 4 oz. bread, 1 oz. cheese.
MON.	broth, 4 oz. bread, 1 oz. cheese.	1 oz. suet in 12 oz. pudding, 1 pint beer.	1 pint milk, 4 oz. bread, 1 oz. cheese.
TUE.	1 pint milk, 4 oz. bread, half oz. butter.	sheep's head and hange between five, 4 oz. bread, 1 pt. beer.	broth, 4 oz. bread, 1 oz. cheese.
WED.	broth, 4 oz. bread, half oz. butter.	1 pint flour milk, 4 oz. bread.	4 oz. bread, 2 oz. cheese, 1 pint beer.
THU.	1 pint milk, 4 oz. bread, half oz. butter.	8 oz. beef or mutton, 4 oz. bread, 1 pint beer, vegetables.	broth, 4 oz. bread, 1 oz. cheese.
FRI.	4 oz. bread, 1 oz. cheese.	1 pint flour milk, 4 oz. bread.	4 oz. bread, 2 oz. cheese, 1 pint beer.
SAT.	1 pint milk, 4 oz. bread, half oz. butter.	1 oz. butter, 1 pint pease, 4 oz. bread, 1 pint beer.	4 oz. bread, 2 oz. cheese, 1 pint beer.

(In winter, milk pottage instead of flour milk, except for pease on Wednesdays. Bread to be wholemeal after extraction of flour for puddings. Beer to be brewed with 3 bushells of malt per hogshead)

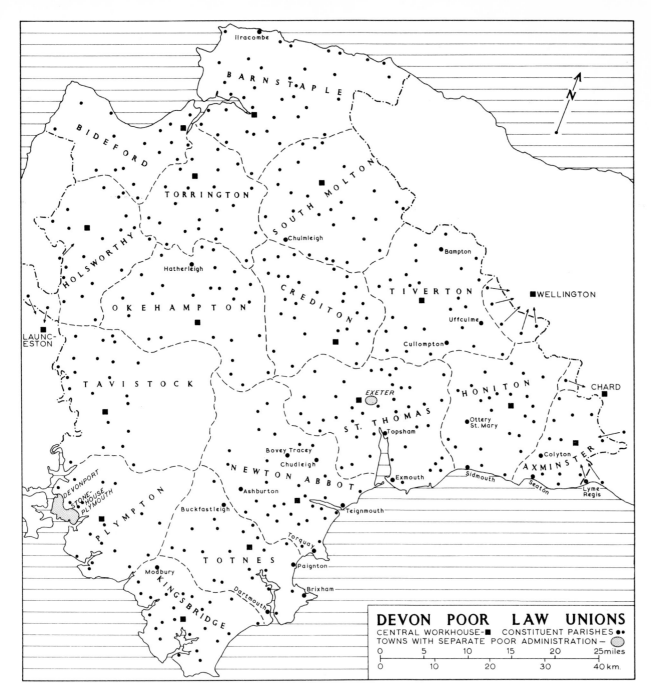

DEVON POOR LAW UNIONS

CENTRAL WORKHOUSE- ■   CONSTITUENT PARISHES ●●
TOWNS WITH SEPARATE POOR ADMINISTRATION - ⬤

0	5	10	15	20	25 miles
0		10	20	30	40 km.

tion of relief. 'Church Houses', often erected in Devon villages about 1500 for various parish purposes, were taken into use for this purpose: and records survive of their stringent rules, running expenses, and diet. But the work required seldom went beyond spinning for women, and gardening or similar tasks for men (if they were able), and never paid much towards costs. With the later eighteenth century the extent of poverty grew too large for parish workhouses, and outdoor relief returned on an increasingly massive scale following the Act of 1796 which authorised payment according to the current price of bread. Nationally, the amount of Poor Rate increased fourfold between then and 1818 – about three times as fast as the population – with the distress caused by, and following, the long Revolutionary and Napoleonic Wars. Nothing was done to change the system until a reforming Whig government followed the Parliamentary Reform of 1832: but action then quickly ensued.

The New Poor Law of 1834, while leaving parishes (until 1865) still rated for their own poor, compelled them to join into Unions, under an elected Board of Guardians, which were to establish Union Workhouses and refuse any relief outside them, while making workhouse life 'less eligible' than that of the poorest independent labourer. This drastic change had the effect, at first, of nearly halving Poor Rates, but at the cost of much human misery. It also, incidentally, abolished Settlement by apprenticeship to a shipmaster or fisherman, or by serving a year's contract service, and gave bastards the Settlement of their mother instead of their parish of birth.

In Devon, sixteen Unions were established, apart from Exeter, Plymouth, Devonport and Stonehouse which were already organised under pre-1834 Acts. Each established its workhouse, replacing the local ones with a central institution with all the economies of scale; though Holsworthy was laggard. White, in 1850, reported the 'Workhouse not yet erected for the Union, but there is a small old Poorhouse in the town'. For convenience, Axminster included three Dorset parishes, and five Devon ones were attached to Wellington. The two beyond the Tamar went to Launceston, and Yarcombe to Chard.

Under the central direction of the Poor Law Board, and later the Local Government Board, policy as to enforcing the 'Workhouse Test' varied in the later nineteenth century. At times outdoor relief was allowed in cases of sickness or old age, and at others refused. In 1865 responsibility for Poor Rate was placed on the Unions as a whole, which evened the burden between richer and poorer parishes: but not till the present century was a start made towards transferring the cost to the national exchequer, with Lloyd George's old-age pensions (1909) and sickness and unemployment insurance for lower-paid workers (1911), followed eventually by the full development of National Insurance (1948). Workhouses were then no longer required, but many survive as hospitals or in other public use. Some were surprisingly well built, and that at Newton Abbot, which cost with its fittings £13 000, was described in the 1850 Directory as 'one of the best in England in external appearance and internal arrangement'.

The Unions, incidentally, formed the basis for local government reform in 1894, when their rural areas became 'Rural Districts' and their town parts 'Urban Districts' – lasting till the changes of 1974.

—20—
NINETEENTH-CENTURY ELEMENTARY SCHOOLS

At the start of the nineteenth century there were many schools in Devon towns and villages, wholly or partly supported by endowments, patrons, subscriptions, or parish rate (or a combination), offering free or subsidised teaching to children whose parents could not meet the full cost. But their quality, and the use actually made of them, was another matter. Teachers in the more solid town schools might have served an apprenticeship by way of training, but in villages they often took on the work for lack of a more profitable alternative and were far from effective. Parish apprenticeship in rural areas took children from school at the age of nine; and before this their attendance was spasmodic, and the teaching usually confined to reading and catechism. For many children there was no chance of schooling, and its value to a future farm labourer was in any case minimal, apart from, perhaps, instilling some respect for religion and authority. But the better town schools went much further in teaching, kept their pupils longer, and had some relevance to future prospects in trade or industry.

Early in the century the 'National Society' (Church) and the 'British Society' (un-

The original National School of Woolfardisworthy, near Hartland. This doubled as a shop, the master displaying stock in the large windows. Not until 1879 was it replaced by a Board School under a qualified master.

denominational, and supported mainly by Dissenters who could not afford a separate school of their own) both pioneered the 'monitorial' system of teaching, by which a teacher could, after a fashion, instruct large numbers by using older pupils as intermediaries to pass on lessons to small groups. But this, while workable in large town schools, had little use in the countryside where there were, in any case, hardly any older pupils to take on the task. Both societies began on a small scale the training of teachers to work the system, and to make small grants in aid of building costs; but their influence in Devon was at first limited, and that of the British Society never considerable outside the larger towns where there was money and influence behind the Dissenters.

Not till 1834 did the Government for the first time intervene to help, and then at first to a very small degree, by offering grants towards the cost of building, through the societies – originally without any guarantee that a school once built could be maintained. But 1839 saw two developments of great future importance: the establishment of the Committee of Council for Education and, on National Society initiative, of the Diocesan Board of Education. The latter was quick to establish the Diocesan Training School (later St Luke's) in Exeter; and the former embarked on a series of

fundamental reforms which were to have a great effect in improving the better schools (but which for many years left the poorly-supported untouched).

Further building grants were made subject to some assurance of future support for a school, and Inspectors were appointed with the duty of visiting those to which such grants had been made. Their reports quickly showed up the great deficiencies of many schools, and led to moves for improvement. 1846 saw the introduction of pupil-teachers, serving a five-year apprenticeship in a school, and paid by Government a salary of £10 rising to £20, with a final examination leading to the award of a Queen's Scholarship for entry to a Training College. The object was both to replace the now discredited monitors and to improve the quality of College entrants. At the same time came Certificate examinations for teachers, offering an addition to salary of £15–30 for men and £10–20 for women, according to grade of certificate, provided school managers paid at least double the amount. Some town schools, particularly the excellent ones in Tiverton under the patronage of the manufacturers Heathcoat and Brewin, were quick to follow up these offers and employ teachers with certificates and pupil-teachers; but in rural Devon the Inspector found only five schools suitable to take pupil-teachers without great improvement first. Next year, ten pence per head of

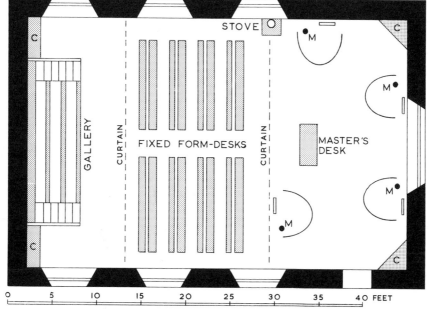

BIDEFORD BRITISH SCHOOL — BOYS SCHOOLROOM

M–MONITOR'S STATION WITH SURROUNDING 'LINES' FOR PUPILS.   C–CUPBOARD
AN EXAMPLE OF LAYOUT FOR THE THREE FORMS OF EARLY 'BRITISH' INSTRUCTION:
GALLERY (SEATS ONLY) FOR CLASS TEACHING NOT INVOLVING WRITING; FORM-DESKS
FOR WRITING; AND SITES FOR MONITORIAL INSTRUCTION OF SMALL GROUPS.

average attendance was offered towards the cost of books and apparatus, if local managers raised twice as much. In 1853 an annual grant was made available to approved rural schools on the number of pupils present for at least 176 days in the year; and three years later this was extended to schools in towns.

All this was intended to aid self-help, and the benefits went consequently only to schools already well-supported – particularly in towns. The effect was to make good schools better, but to leave bad ones (particularly in villages) as bad as before. It also meant a great increase in national expenditure on education, and greatly complicated the work of the Committee of Council: and the result was the drastic cut-back of the 1863 Revised Code. This ended State salaries for pupil-teachers and payments to teachers with certificates, and reduced building grants. Henceforth there was to be only one annual payment, direct to the managers, and based on the number of passes in six Standards for reading, writing and arithmetic, plus a flat rate for infants if approved. The immediate results were predictable: far fewer boys came forward as pupil-teachers, and those who completed their apprenticeship often took work outside teaching; the number of men entrants to Training Colleges fell nationally to under sixty per cent, and thenceforth more women were employed as teachers – having, unlike men, little alternative. The income of certificated teachers was at once cut, and, even after a general addition of a share of the earned grant, was lower than before; and remaining pupil-teachers, now paid direct by managers, received on average only about two-thirds of the previous salary.

The need to concentrate on the 3Rs meant the general abandonment of other subjects, and the need to examine each child individually reduced the work of the Inspector to a mechanical drudgery. In 1866 the average salary of masters appointed from St Luke's was £60 plus a house – the lowest of all Training Colleges, and considerably less than before with the Government payment. A further result was a proliferation of 3R Night Schools, for adolescents whose day schooling had been inadequate, in the hope of supplementing a meagre salary with the grant so earned; but in rural areas this was often pathetically small.

Most rural schools, however, were still unaffected because they had never qualified for any form of grant; and an enquiry in 1870 found that Bideford and Holsworthy Unions had less than half the school places they required, and only eight per cent in

RULES OF THE
PEHEMBURY NATIONAL SCHOOL.

ADMISSION.

Children may be admitted any Monday morning, at a quarter before Nine o'Clock, under the following conditions, viz.— that the parents or guardians undertake to observe the following Rules.

ATTENDANCE.

On Sunday, children to assemble in the morning at half-past 9, afternoon at quarter to 2 o'Clock.

On Week-days, children to assemble quarter before 9 o'Clock, and in the afternoon at quarter to 2 o'Clock.

A child who comes late will have a mark on the Register.

School hours from 9 to 12, and from 2 to 4.

Children must be sent clean and neat in person and dress, or will have to be sent home

Children will be required to learn lessons at home in winter.

PAYMENTS, to be made in advance.

Labourers to pay 1s a quarter for each child ; Tradesmen 1s 6d. Double the above rates for such as write in copy books.

Parents who do not send their children to School when they can do so, will lose the privileges of the **Clothing Club,** and other Charities for themselves.

If three children of the same family, a small reduction will be made in the payments.

The school treat and prizes will depend on regular attendance.

All children above six years of age, residing in the Parish and attending the Day School, will be expected to be present on Sundays.

G. SWEETMAN, BOOKSELLER, WINCANTON.

Note early spelling of Payhembury (1851)

grant-earning schools. Honiton had only three per cent in the latter category, and only in St Thomas and Tavistock was the figure over thirty per cent. The result was the famous 1870 Education Act, by which the State changed its policy from only helping better schools to requiring positive provision of places in 'efficient' schools for all of school age. All schools were to have certificated headteachers who could earn a grant. The sudden increase in the need for such teachers was to some extent met by allowing a 'Provisional Certificate' for approved former pupil-teachers who could take direct charge of a small school at the age of eighteen and continue, provided they got their certificate by examination by twenty-five. Certificates could also be given without examination to approved established headteachers. The Act also required sufficient school places to be provided, either by voluntary means, with the help of a building grant if needed, and by raising funds for maintenance by subscriptions or Voluntary Rate, or by a School Board which could raise a compulsory rate and borrow on mortgage from the Public Works Loan Commission for a new or extended building.

Outside towns, the effects were much slower than expected or intended, since parishes nearly all tried to remain 'Voluntary' to save expense, and four or five years elapsed before the Education Department lost patience with those who failed to deliver, and compelled a Board to be formed. Devon in fact had more compulsorily formed School Boards than any other county, and eventually there were 91 of them serving populations of under 1000, of which 39 were for places with fewer than 500, and 9 with fewer than 250! In these, and particularly the last, it was often hard to find people with any interest in education to

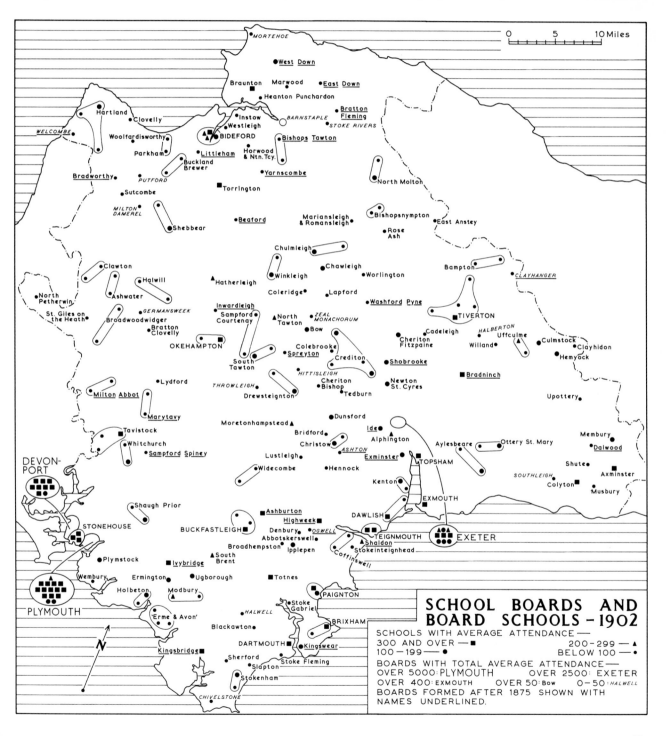

SCHOOL BOARDS AND BOARD SCHOOLS – 1902

SCHOOLS WITH AVERAGE ATTENDANCE —
300 AND OVER — ■   200 - 299 — ▲
100 - 199 — ●   BELOW 100 — •
BOARDS WITH TOTAL AVERAGE ATTENDANCE —
OVER 5000 : PLYMOUTH   OVER 2500 : EXETER
OVER 400 : EXMOUTH   OVER 50 : Bow   0 - 50 : HALWELL
BOARDS FORMED AFTER 1875 SHOWN WITH
NAMES UNDERLINED.

stand, and many rural Boards came to be dominated by farmers whose chief concern was to keep the rates low, and whose sympathy for the education of their future labourers was minimal.

In the towns it was very different, and most towns of any size, except Torquay (which was generously provided with Voluntary schools), soon formed a Board with a real concern for education. While the record of rural School Boards varied from the respectable to the abysmal, town Boards quickly fulfilled the aims of the Act and went further, earning a reputation as generous pioneers. The Plymouth and Devonport Boards both founded Higher Grade Schools, the former with a large science department; and the Exeter Board earned from HMI in 1894 the comment that it was 'generous to its schools, keeps a good staff, rewards pupils with prizes, has established a small library for teachers, and has a system of personal visiting'.

Tiverton Board was exceptionally generous to the several rural schools in its large area; and all enforced their attendance bye-laws – which rural Boards and Union Attendance Committees never did, largely because of the refusal of rural magistrates to convict. Plymouth set up a 'Truants Industrial School' to house and discipline those who wilfully evaded teaching, and offered places in it to other Boards, which some towns (but hardly any villages) made use of. Plymouth, Devonport, Exeter and Barnstaple all set up Pupil-Teacher Centres, as did the Torbay towns, which were of great benefit to those within reach, but again left the rural pupil-teacher in isolation. Figures for 1900 show that in large Devon towns the Board schools were much better supported than surviving Voluntary ones, but the reverse applied in the countryside. In fact, in towns there was a demand for education as a way to better employment, while in villages the prospect for nearly all boys was still only farm-labouring, and for girls domestic service before marriage to a labourer.

Voluntary schools continued to be the majority in Devon as a whole, and in villages they were nearly all 'Church', since rural Nonconformity, however widespread, had little wealth to back it. These in turn varied greatly in local support and interest. Towards the end of the century, in 1897, the poorer ones were much helped by 'New Aid Grant', paid through the Societies for raising salaries, increasing staff, or for equipment. Some indeed were, by 1900, receiving more than ninety per cent of their total costs from various Government grants. These in-

cluded the Fee Grant of ten shillings per head which replaced School Pence in 1891, 'small population' grant, grant for adequate staffing, besides earned grant – all, apart from Aid Grant, also available to Board schools.

The Code governing curriculum and grant, which had been designed with large town schools in mind where every Standard could have a separate teacher, sat hard on rural schools where one teacher might have to take all the Standards – and sometimes the infants as well. In practice most rural children left school at the age of ten if they could scrape through Standard IV, which somewhat lessened the problem, and School Pence scales were often designed to force them out into the fields at that age. There was gradual liberalisation in the addition of grant for singing – compared by one North Devon HMI with the noise made by a distressed family begging in the street – and for 'Class Subjects' such as history, geography and grammar (which in fact were little more than rote-learning of little understood information). A seventh Standard – irrelevant in the rural school – was introduced in 1882; and in 1891 the 3R inspection was dropped, to the great relief of both teachers and Inspectors. Finally in 1900 the last vestige of 'Payment by Results' vanished with a single block-grant on average attendance.

By the end of the century the inadequacy of the rural parish – and particularly of the rural School Board – as a separate 'education authority' was obvious; and the Act of 1902 (effective in 1903) transferred responsibility for maintaining both Voluntary and Board schools (outside Plymouth–Devonport, Exeter, Torquay, Barnstaple and Tiverton) to the County Council which could draw on the rates of richer areas to lighten the burden on the poorer. But despite its rural limitations, much had been achieved since the 1870 Act.

For the great majority of country children the result was little more than some grounding in social discipline, the ability to read the less demanding newspapers, to write (if with a limited vocabulary), and to work simple sums: but this alone was a great advance. For a few, in the better schools, pupil-teacher apprenticeship offered a way into teaching. Otherwise, escape from wretchedly paid farm or domestic work was probably dependent on the chance of craft-apprenticeship or migration. There was more opportunity in country towns, with a wider variety of employment and less parental poverty to compel early leaving, and occasionally the chance of a scholarship to further education.

—21—
POPULATION GROWTH AND DISTRIBUTION SINCE 1801

When the first Census was taken in 1801, Devon had some 340,000 people out of a total for Britain of about 10½ million. This was well up to the national average for a time before the Industrial Revolution had made much mark outside a few limited areas, and when density still mainly depended on agriculture. By 1851 there were 567 000, an increase of sixty-seven per cent, but meanwhile the population of the whole country had risen by nearly a hundred per cent. The great industrial towns, based on coal, which had grown elsewhere, had no counterpart in Devon: instead, their competition was helping to extinguish what remained of industry in the county. But agriculture was still very flourishing, and apart from the port towns and Exeter it still governed the distribution of population in Devon. Railways had as yet had little time to make their effects felt; and though the total in places of over 3000 had grown much faster than that of the villages, much of it was still in market towns whose fortunes mainly depended on farming.

The 1851 map shows all places which then had over 1000 people: and one striking fact that it illustrates is that there were twice as many large villages between 1000 and 2000 as there were a century later. Labourers' wages were abominably low in Devon, even by the standards of the time, and farmers could afford to employ as many as they could find a use for. At this stage they were about seven to eight shillings a week in North Devon, and eight to nine in the south. Though the more enterprising villagers sometimes moved off to seek better fortune elsewhere, this was much more difficult than it later became. The prosperity of farming in turn supported markets, tradesmen and craftsmen in the small inland towns.

The next fifty years saw Devon's population rise by under seventeen per cent, while the country as a whole increased by seventy-seven per cent. Such increase as there was, was urban, and in the countryside there was actually a steep fall. Many villages and small market towns lost a quarter or a third of their people, and some villages more than forty per cent, after farming ran into the great depression from the 1870s with the competition of cheap imported grain. Much land previously under cereals

had to be turned over to stock-grazing, with consequently less demand for labour; and falling income also obliged farmers to manage with fewer men and less lavish spending in the market town. The areas hardest hit were the less fertile soils of the north and north-west, where the 1951 map shows significant blank spaces compared with that for 1851. Railways, as already mentioned, sometimes actually hastened the decline of the smaller market centres.

In 1863 Edward Girdlestone came to Halberton as Vicar, from Lancashire where farm-workers (thanks to alternative employment in industry) were much better paid and housed. His attempts to persuade the local farmers to give them fairer treatment met only open hostility, and from 1866 till he left in 1872 he applied the classic remedy of decreasing the supply of labour to increase its price. He organised and helped the migration of over 400 men, some with families, to Kent and to northern counties, and those who prospered encouraged others to follow. So began a great movement, followed by emigration to the United States and the British colonies, which drained many rural Devon parishes. From the 1870s onwards there was also a considerable movement from North Devon to South Wales, where industrial employment could be found, helped by the close trading connections by coaster across the Bristol Channel. Partly as a result, by the end of the century farm-workers' wages had risen to 12–13 shillings a week – though they were still low by comparison with most other counties.

By 1900 the mines of Tavistock and the Dartmoor fringes were worked out, and the last rural woollen mills had succumbed to the competition of better organised large-scale ones in the north, helped by local coal. The only considerable forms of alternative labour in country districts had therefore ceased: and the large estates, feeling the pinch of agricultural depression, dismissed labour on a locally disastrous scale in the 1890s. By 1900, therefore, the self-contained village communities with their abundant shops and craftsmen, so evident in the 1850 Directory, were fast waning.

Along the south coast the situation was very different. Holiday resorts, which were also favoured for retirement, had grown out of all proportion. Torquay more than doubled, and Paignton trebled, its size in this half-century. The Plymouth towns also nearly doubled as the port and dockyard developed; and the railway and industrial centre of Newton Abbot (which had been a small market town

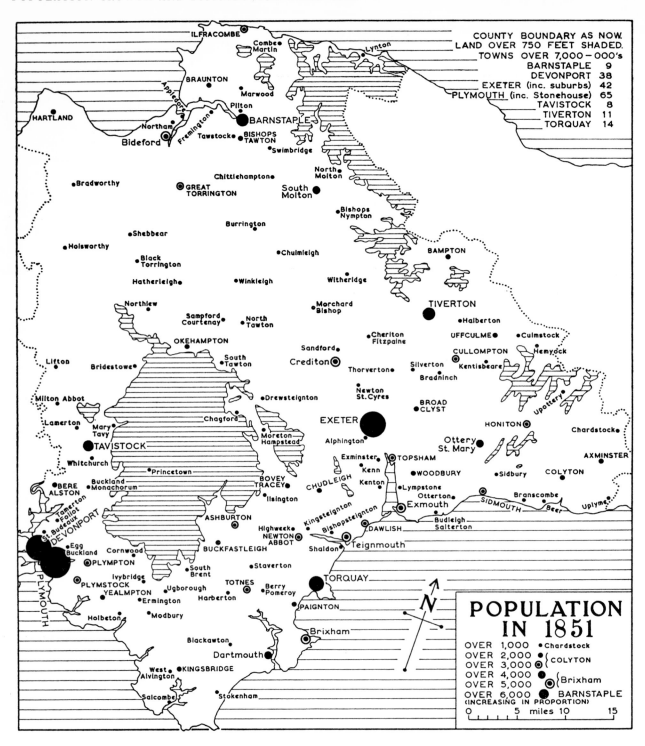

before the railway arrived) had outstripped Tiverton and Barnstaple.

The half-century before 1951 for the most part continued the trends which developed in the later nineteenth century. Except during the First World War, farming remained depressed: and the revival after 1939 coincided with mechanisation and a steady rise in the cost of labour, and consequently made little difference to the numbers employed. Inland villages barely held their own, or declined still further, unless they had some other source of employment like a factory or quarry. The devel-

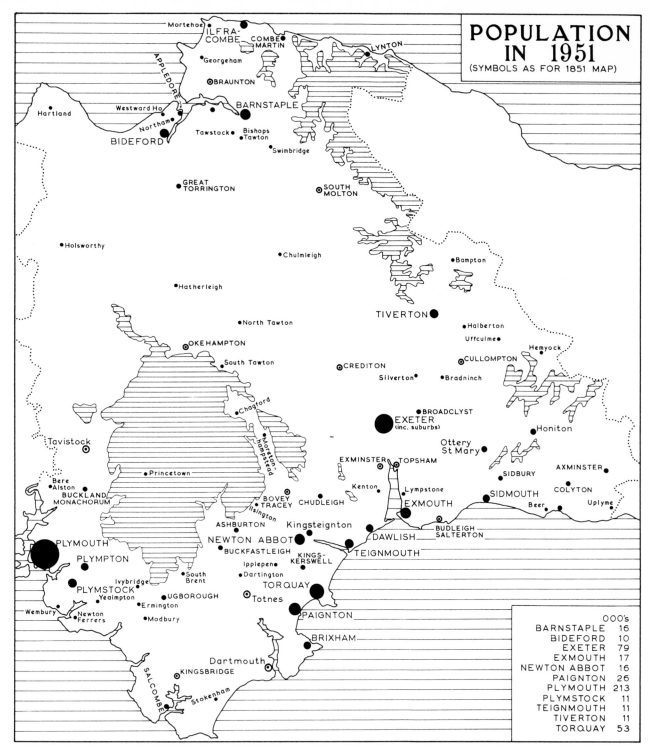

POPULATION
IN 1951
(SYMBOLS AS FOR 1851 MAP)

	000's
BARNSTAPLE	16
BIDEFORD	10
EXETER	79
EXMOUTH	17
NEWTON ABBOT	16
PAIGNTON	26
PLYMOUTH	213
PLYMSTOCK	11
TEIGNMOUTH	11
TIVERTON	11
TORQUAY	53

opment of bus and car transport, however, made it easier for people to live at a distance from their work, and some villages near large towns had grown as a result. On the other hand, the trade of smaller inland centres suffered still further. Urbanisation continued to the point when nearly half the total population lived in Plymouth (including Devonport since 1914), Exeter, and the Torbay towns, and over seventy per cent in places with more than 3000 people.

The thirty years since 1951 have however seen a marked reversal of some previous trends, and a great

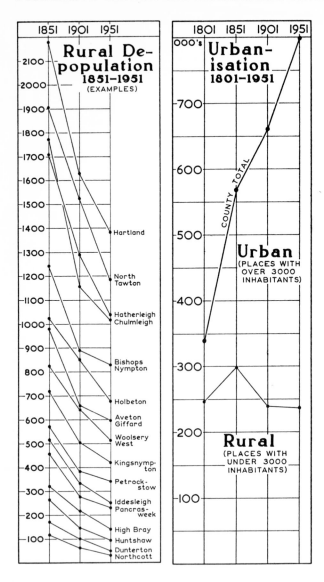

Tiverton and Tavistock have also grown by over fifty per cent, and the resort towns Exmouth and Dawlish by, respectively, over fifty per cent and forty per cent.

Private car ownership has meant the run-down or extinction of rural public transport, and a consequent distinction between mobile car-owners, as commuters or with easy access to towns for other purposes, and the rest – mostly the less affluent local workers or pensioners – who are more isolated than before. With few exceptions, increased village population has not resulted from increased local employment; and the effect has been the introduction of newcomers with a generally higher living-standard than that of indigenous people, and consequently something of a social division in previously homogeneous village societies.

Exeter and Plymouth have both had boundary extensions, the latter taking in Plympton and Plymstock, making Exeter over 95 000 and Plymouth over 241 000; but many of those working in either place live in a neighbouring village. Ivybridge (not even a parish until 1894), because of its nearness to the latter, increased its population in these thirty years from 1852 to 5106, not far short of the ancient town of Totnes!

development of the already noticeable effect on 'commuter' villages near large towns. Though rural population in the less accessible or less attractive parts of the county has remained stable or actually declined still further, the massive growth in private car ownership with post-1951 'affluence' has caused a striking population increase in many villages. Much of this new settlement is of people who work in towns, or of retired incomers seeking a pleasant place to live after a life's work in the great conurbations of the Midlands and London. Previously declining country towns have also in most cases recovered – Crediton by over fifty per cent and Torrington and Honiton by over forty per cent. Semi-industrialised Newton Abbot has grown by over forty per cent and its neighbouring contributors Kingsteignton and the Kerswells by still more.

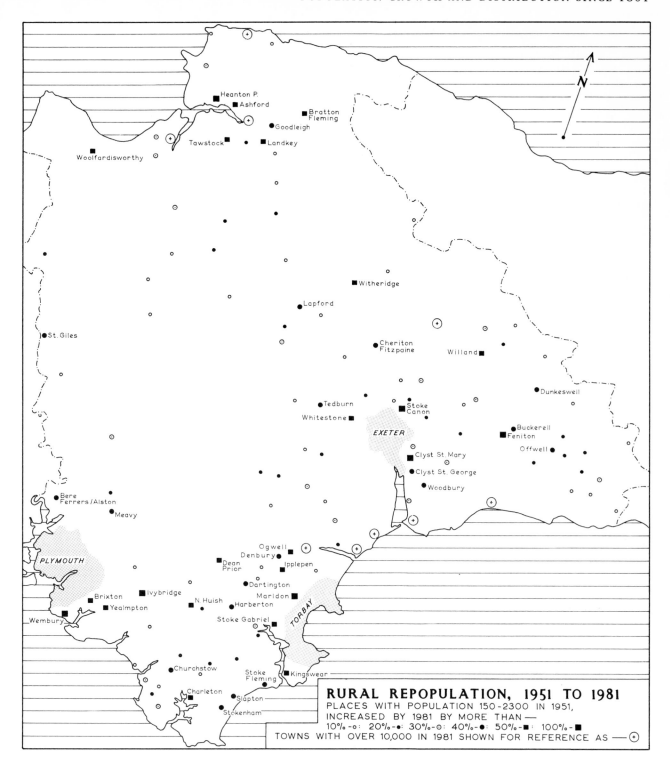

N

Heanton P.
Ashford
Bratton
Fleming
Goodleigh
Tawstock
Landkey
Woolfardisworthy

Witheridge

Lapford

St. Giles

Cheriton
Fitzpaine
Willand

Dunkeswell

Tedburn
Whitestone
Stoke
Canon
EXETER

Buckerell
Feniton
Offwell

Clyst St. Mary

Clyst St. George
Woodbury

Bere
Ferrers/Alston
Meavy

Ogwell
Denbury
Dean
Prior
Ipplepen

PLYMOUTH

Dartington
Brixton   Ivybridge
Marldon
Yealmpton   N. Huish
Harberton
Wembury
Stoke Gabriel
TORBAY

Churchstow
Stoke
Fleming   Kingswear
Charleton

RURAL REPOPULATION, 1951 TO 1981
PLACES WITH POPULATION 150-2300 IN 1951,
INCREASED BY 1981 BY MORE THAN —
10%-○: 20%-•: 30%-◎: 40%-●: 50%-■: 100%-■
TOWNS WITH OVER 10,000 IN 1981 SHOWN FOR REFERENCE AS — ⊕

Slapton
Stokenham

INDEX